## Jeff Taylor

Recognized as an innovator and visionary in both the Internet and careers industries, Jeff Taylor has reinvented the way the world looks for employment. His "monster idea," conceived at the dawn of the World Wide Web, quickly became one of the first dot-com companies (454th on the Web) and has since grown into the world's leading online career site. Today, the Monster global network consists of local content and language sites in twenty-three countries and serves more than 50 million registered users, with over 20 million unique visitors monthly.

Jeff is a frequent speaker at colleges and universities across the country, and at technology, advertising, and human capital conferences hosted by such noted organizations as Forrester Research, 21st Century Workforce Summit, The Partnership for Public Service, The Society for Human Resource Management (SHRM), Fast Company, and The Working Women Network. He serves on both the national and Massachusetts boards of directors of Junior Achievement and is also a board member of Boston's Wang Center for the Performing Arts.

Jeff has an undergraduate degree from the University of Massachusetts at Amherst and a certificate from the Owner/President Management (OPM) Program, Executive Education, Harvard Business School. He also holds an honorary doctorate from Bentley College.

In March 2000, Jeff reached yet another notable milestone: he became the Blimp Water-skiing World Champion.

## Doug Hardy

Doug Hardy, a certified job and career transition coach, was the editor in chief of Monster and is currently general manager of Monster Careers. Prior to joining Monster, Hardy directed book, magazine, and Web publishing businesses in New York and Boston.

Both Taylor and Hardy live near Boston.

# monster®
## Careers:

# INTERVIEWING

Master the Moment That Gets You the Job

BY JEFF TAYLOR,
FOUNDER OF **monster**®
WITH DOUG HARDY

PENGUIN BOOKS

PENGUIN BOOKS
Published by the Penguin Group
Penguin Group (USA) Inc., 375 Hudson Street, New York, New York 10014, U.S.A.
Penguin Group (Canada), 90 Eglinton Avenue East, Suite 700, Toronto, Ontario,
Canada M4P 2Y3 (a division of Pearson Penguin Canada Inc.)
Penguin Books Ltd, 80 Strand, London WC2R 0RL, England
Penguin Ireland, 25 St Stephen's Green, Dublin 2, Ireland (a division of Penguin
Books Ltd)
Penguin Group (Australia), 250 Camberwell Road, Camberwell, Victoria 3124,
Australia (a division of Pearson Australia Group Pty Ltd)
Penguin Books India Pvt Ltd, 11 Community Centre, Panchsheel Park,
New Delhi–110 017, India
Penguin Group (NZ), cnr Airborne and Rosedale Roads, Albany, Auckland 1310,
New Zealand (a division of Pearson New Zealand Ltd)
Penguin Books (South Africa) (Pty) Ltd, 24 Sturdee Avenue, Rosebank, Johannesburg
2196, South Africa

Penguin Books Ltd, Registered Offices:
80 Strand, London WC2R 0RL, England

First published in Penguin Books 2005

10  9  8  7  6  5  4  3  2  1

Copyright © Monster Worldwide, 2005
All rights reserved

CIP data available
ISBN 0-14-303577-0

Printed in the United States of America
Set in Giovanni
Designed by Heather Saunders

# CONTENTS

# DEDICATION AND ACKNOWLEDGMENTS

*For Ryan, Brooke, and Cole*
—J.T.

*For Emilie, Will, and Sprint*
—D.H.

I'd like to extend grateful thanks to Monster's employer customers (and friends) who shared their stories and insights on the job interview process: Marie Artim, Wendy Babson, Mark Bidwell, John Caffrey, Ian Christie, Lisa Cornay-Albright, Patti Cotter, Jeevan DeVore, Michael Durik, Carmine Gallo, Brian Gard, Glen Goodman, Lorelei Grazier, Dan Gregory, Steve Harper, Jill Harris, Felix Heimberg, Bill Hickmott, Kate M. Kavanagh, Sean Kavanagh, Kristin Kohler, Eric Lee, Carole Martin, Tom Montgomery, Ed Newman, Christie Peacock, Jennifer M. Scott, Carol Szatkowski, John Swanson, Matthew Temple, David Trance, Peter Vogt, Donald Weintraub, Jackie Wimmer, and Frank E. Wittenauer.

Thanks again to Monster's agent and trusted advisor, Peter Ginsberg of Curtis Brown, Ltd, and to our excellent editors Jane von Mehren and Brett Kelly. Thanks also to their ever-professional colleagues at Curtis Brown and Penguin.

Many Monster employees gave their time and enthusiasm to the creation of this book and its companion, *Monster Careers: How to Land the Job of Your Life*—too many, in fact, to list here! Thanks to them and all Monster employees for making Monster an exceptional place to "earn, learn, and yearn"—every day.

# INTRODUCTION

Imagine a typical job interview at about the 20-minute mark. One of two scenes is usually taking place:

In one scene, the candidate appears nervous. The interviewer is noncommittal. The talk is more question-and-answer about the candidate's resume rather than real conversation about the job. See that look of self-doubt in the candidate's eyes? It's a sure sign that he or she hasn't made a real connection with the interviewer. Not good.

In the second scene, the candidate is sitting forward, with bright eyes and a relaxed, alert expression. He or she is answering and asking questions eagerly, carrying on a confident conversation with the interviewer. The interviewer not only remembers their name, but is already imagining that name on the company roster. The next forty minutes of conversation are going to be great.

Most interviews get to a point where they tip toward or away from the candidate. When they tip away, a kind of downward spiral sets in; the candidate probably isn't going to get the job. When they tip toward the candidate, I call that the Monster moment—suddenly the interviewer has a clear picture of the candidate in the job. He starts asking questions that reinforce his positive view. The conversation moves from a review of resume items to a high-level conversation about the business.

*Monster Careers: Interviewing* will train you to make sure that when you reach that moment, you will be well on your way to getting the job—if you want it. Twenty minutes into the interview, you will be thinking, "Wow, I feel good. I'm getting my messages across; I'm building rapport with the interviewer, and now they're asking me to keep talking. This is great!"

Anybody can give a strong interview performance . . . *anybody*. If you know what the person on the other side of the desk really wants—and why—you can transform your nervous energy into confident enthusiasm.

Follow the advice in this book and you'll be at your best during the one hour that moves you toward the job of your dreams.

You'll lay a foundation for a good interview performance with an up-to-date understanding of the fundamentals:

- Landing the interview in the first place.
- Practicing your main "selling points" so that you can present them confidently.
- Putting together the appearance, behaviors, and attitude that say, "this is a professional."

Along the way, you'll learn surprising truths about job interviews such as:

- Interviewers are often as nervous and inexperienced as you.
- Interviewers tend to fall into "types," for which you can adjust your style.
- The format of the interview can determine how you'll answer questions.
- Interviewers play games (whether they mean to or not!).

To wrap up your training, you'll find great answers to more than five hundred job interview questions, along with insights into what the interviewer is looking for from each of them.

Throughout the book, there are great tips and stories from human resources professionals under the heading "My Best Advice," as well as incredible-but-true stories of terrible interview mistakes, under the heading "What Were They Thinking?"

There are three ways to use this book:

- If you have an urgent need to study (a job interview tomorrow for example), check out "What If Your Interview Is Tomorrow?" on pages 1–5.
- If you have time, read the book from front to back. The chapters are arranged in chronological order—getting interviews, preparing for them, and following up after them. These are all crucial steps to getting a great job.
- If you want to find descriptions and suggested answers to specific interview questions, see the question index on page 211.

*Monster Careers: Interviewing* contains several simple exercises that will help you put what you've learned into action. You need to invest some time in these exercises! There is no substitute or shortcut for hard work up front, preparing for the interview.

Since interviewing involves distinct roles for people and organizations, I've used the following labels:

- A *candidate* is someone applying for a job (occasionally I'll also use the more generic-sounding term *job seeker*).
- An *interviewer* is anyone interviewing a candidate for a job—a manager or human resources director, for example.
- An *employer* or *company* is the organization you'll work for, including any kind of employer—private, public, nonprofit, government, you name it.
- A *recruiter* plays an intermediary role between you and the employer. Also called a headhunter, a recruiter's job is to find likely candidates for a job—and they conduct some interviews—but they do not make the final hiring decision.

Monster keeps a Web site dedicated to its books at **www.monster careers.com**. There, you'll find additional interview questions, more advice, and great downloadable tools for this book and for our original, comprehensive job search program, *Monster Careers: How to Land the Job of Your Life.*

With the advice and tools in this book, you'll experience that Monster moment for yourself. You'll become the candidate whose name they'll remember; the one who got the job.

—Jeff Taylor

# What If Your Interview Is Tomorrow?

Did you open this book because your job interview is tomorrow morning? If that's the case, you don't have time to take advantage of all the advice in two hundred pages. Follow this action plan tonight, and you'll still be ahead of the game.

**Step 1:** Find out as much as you comfortably can about the interview. Call your contact at the employer and ask:

- Who will you be talking to?
- What's the dress code? (Hint: Dress a little better than they suggest.)
- Are there any special directions for getting there, such as a special place to park or a nearby bus stop?
- What are their expectations for the day? Is it one interview, or will you continue through multiple interviews?
- Can they e-mail you a detailed job description?

**Step 2:** Do some quick research. Go to the employer's Web site, and note a couple of items to discuss. For example: "Last week you launched a new product. What's the marketing plan for that?" Do a search on Yahoo! Finance or Google to get the latest news. If the company is publicly held, study what investors say about the company's stock. Write down a few facts: How big is the company? Where is the headquarters? What are its top business lines?

Read the boilerplate at the bottom of press releases the company has published. This information is the minimum that they feel they should be communicating in every single release, so you should know it.

**Step 3:** Complete the exercise called "Mastering the Freestyle Interview" on pages 3–5. This will give you something to say during the trickiest parts of the interview. (You can return to this exercise after you've completed the book.)

**Step 4:** Lay out your interview outfit tonight (see "Dress the Part" on page 184, Chapter 13).

**Step 5:** Get a good night's sleep and leave for your interview a little early.

Good luck—and when you're done with the interview, come back and finish the book!

# EXERCISE

## Mastering the Freestyle Interview

If somebody asks you a fact-finding question, you know how to answer it. Questions about your skills are relatively straightforward as
well. It's the open-ended questions—what I call rapport, culture,
storytelling, and achievement questions—that tend to get unprepared candidates in trouble.

This exercise prepares you for those open-ended questions, which
I call the "freestyle interview." Freestyle because usually there isn't
one single "right" answer. Freestyle because they may be asked at
any time.

Building rapport in an interview requires more than talking
about the weather. You want to drop clues about your cultural fit
with the organization, such as shared values, leadership, and teamwork styles. You want to show strong qualities in your nonwork life,
such as diligence and a "yearn to learn."

For both building rapport and handling stressful questions, you
want to have achievement stories at the ready that prove your claims.
You'll learn more about these stories in chapters 6, 7, and 8, but as
part of your quick study, try writing them down now.

This exercise helps you establish a disciplined approach to your
interview preparation. I urge you to fill out this form completely. If
you're really serious about beating your competition, go beyond the
limits of the printed page and either copy this form several times to
expand your repertoire of talking points, or download an expand-
able version of this form at **monstercareers.com.**

# RAPPORT AND CULTURE

A work achievement that shows a personal quality relevant to the job:

_____

A nonwork achievement that shows a personal quality relevant to the job:

_____

Cultural connections between me and the organization:

Shared values: _____

Shared work style: _____

Shared leadership style: _____

Shared team values: _____

What I am passionate about: _____

What gets me excited: _____

What turns me off: _____

What types of problems I enjoy solving: _____

# STORYTELLING

**Work achievement story #1—my best achievement.**

Problem: _____

Action: _____

Resolution: _____

Value to the business: _____

**Work achievement story #2—another great achievement.**

Problem: _____

Action: _____

Resolution: _____

Value to the business: _____

**Work achievement story #3—an achievement made under pressure.**

Problem: _____

Action: _____

Resolution: _____

Value to the business: _____

**Nonwork achievement story:**

Problem: _____

Action: _____

Resolution: _____

Value to the business: _____

**You can download this form at monstercareers.com.**

**H**ow long have you been in transition?"

"About eight months," said Dave. He hated that term, "in transition." Why didn't interviewers just ask, "How long since you lost your job?"

"Been looking all that time?" asked Susan, the HR director, across her desk.

"I took a couple of months off after my position as office manager was cut," said Dave, quickly adding, "It was summer and nobody was hiring. I've been applying for jobs since September." Dave could feel himself shrinking into his hard plastic chair. "I've had several interviews, mostly with office parks along the beltway."

"I see," said Susan, jotting a note on Dave's resume. "Let's talk for a few minutes about your qualifications. . . ."

Wow, this feels just like the last two interviews, thought Dave. They ask the same questions, and I give the same answers. I was a facilities and office manager for the Triangle Office Park, blah, blah, blah. When two of the anchor tenants had to leave, the office management company had to let me go, blah, blah. They gave me three weeks' pay and some nice recommendations. Et cetera.

Dave noticed a photograph of two school-age children on Susan's desk. The younger girl looked about the same age as his boy.

Susan continued her review of Dave's resume. Dave's nervous energy diminished into the predictable slow interview cadence, and then a familiar exasperation. Look, he wanted to say, I know how to do this job, I've done it before, and you advertised for an office manager. Here's my resume. What else is there to talk about? Yet the interview droned on: question-answer; question-answer. He knew he would be great in this job, but how could he convince her of that?

Susan asked, "What would you consider your greatest accomplishment?"

Dave searched his memory, energy still flagging. He wasn't going to get this job. "Um, I can tell you about my last big office move. . . ."

Susan wrote another note, and then looked quickly at the small clock on her desk. Dave stopped.

"You know," said Dave, "I'd rather tell you something else." Surprised by the frankness in his voice, Dave straightened.

"My greatest accomplishment wasn't at work, but when I ran a fund-raiser for the Gillespie day school last year. I could tell you all about organizing parents, staff, and benefactors, and raising more money than any previous year.

"I can also tell you about putting myself through school after my parents' restaurant went out of business. I think of that as a great accomplishment, too."

Dave closed his notebook on the desk, and placed his hand palm down on the cover. "Come to think of it, I would consider landing a new job right now to be a great accomplishment. To do that, I need to tell you something in the next ten minutes that separates me from other candidates."

She smiled and put down her pen, and asked, "Tell me why you think raising money for a day school is like managing three office buildings."

Well, thought Dave, she's not throwing me out yet. Maybe we can just have a conversation. He opened his notebook, glanced at the job description, and said, "Okay. Let's talk about organization skills. . . ."


Job interviews can be a dance of mutual frustration.

You muster a big effort and then wonder why you didn't make a great impression. The interviewer wonders how to get a clear picture of you—are you "the one"?—in less than an hour. Too often, the interview becomes more about why you *shouldn't* get the job than why you *should*. Too often, the closing remarks tell the story: They say, "We'll get back to you." Then they continue looking . . . and so do you.

You might picture a job interview as a police interrogation, with the all-powerful interviewer firing questions at you, the helpless candidate. Many interviewers are also this negative. They think there's a system to interviewing, as if it could be mastered and repeated like a card trick. Their misunderstanding results in second-rate hiring for them, and for you, no forward progress in your search for the ideal job.

You don't have to fall into this trap. There's another way to look at the job interview, a bigger way, one that doesn't just imagine that single anxious interrogation but instead sees job interviews as an ever-expanding web of conversation including:

- Your skills, experience, career decisions; your character and values.
- Any potential employer's needs, business plans, and culture.
- Anyone who can connect you to a job, whether or not they're hiring.

That's the career-centered conversation I call a **Monster Interview.** It's a competency you acquire and refine throughout your career, not just when you're looking for a job. The Monster Interview is your life-long conversation with the job market; it's a critical component of great career management.

In the story you just read, Dave became so frustrated he went "off script" and interrupted the flow of a typical interview. Dave was fortunate that Susan responded by shifting her routine to a more open, give-and-take conversation. Luckily, Dave's frustration—and preparation—began that real conversation.

The choice is yours—do it the traditional way, and trust the system, or learn to create *your* conversation.

Your side of the conversation comes down to four objectives:

1. Build a positive relationship with the interviewer.
2. Prove you can do the job.
3. Make yourself memorable in comparison with other candidates.
4. Show your potential for leadership and growth.

*Monster Careers: Interviewing* is about getting to your goals: a job offer, a start date, and a great job! Beyond that, your strong performance in a job interview lays the foundation for success later in the job, because during that critical hour, both employer and candidate begin their professional relationship. You want to get off to a great start.

## At Work, You're Always Interviewing

Most careers today require constant communication. This is as true in so-called simple jobs, like waiting tables, as it is in the "knowledge marketplace," where technology makes teamwork essential. We depend more on each other to do our jobs well, and strong communication is the link between interdependent jobs.

It's all about asking the right questions and getting the right answers.

Recognizing this, the best employers I know don't interview people just when they're hiring. They have long-term interview habits that make the hiring process neverending; habits like:

**Informal interviews:** Managers meet with their employees one-to-one to discuss their performance. Sometimes this is about whether or not the employee gets a raise, and sometimes it's a simple "how are you doing?" To excel at this critical moment, keep a private record of your accomplishments, of your skills and work experiences. The first day on your new job, mark your calendar six months from your start date. And when that day comes, *do it:* take a few evenings to assemble your list of skills, experiences, and achievements. Your success depends on habits like this!

Other informal interviews happen in the course of business, for example, when a new opportunity comes up at your current employer. With that private record, you'll be able to make a more compelling case that you should be promoted. When a new boss arrives, you'll be ready with a sensational answer to "what do you do?"

**Outside interviews:** The best managers stay in touch with their business outside their immediate employer. They go to conferences, networking events, schools, and other places where people in their business gather. They ask questions and listen.

**Top-grading interviews:** Top grading is a recent phenomenon in which managers identify their best and worst performers, reward the best and improve or weed out the less successful. Over time, the idea is to build a workforce entirely composed of top-grade employees.

**Exit interviews:** Many employers interview people as they leave the company. These interviews often take place because an employee has found another opportunity, but might also take place because he or she has been laid off. This is a time when many employees are very candid, and where an employer can learn some painful truths.

Actually, you might find yourself in one of these interviews without warning. It starts as a conversation with your boss, and suddenly you realize that this is an exit interview in the making. In the interest of keeping your job, you should be prepared to discuss your value then and there.

In today's job market, opportunities for that Monster moment appear in unexpected places. When you meet someone from an interesting organization at a party, you can do much more than tell them your job title—you can make them think, "I gotta get this person working with me!" In fact, this is the essence of career networking.

The average job these days lasts about three years, so changing jobs is inevitable. You can try to achieve success by gearing up every time for a new set of job interviews, or you can weave these conversations into your daily work life, and find that you are always prepared for a transition.

## Confidence

The Monster Interview is about *confidence*, which comes from the conviction that you are taking the right steps now to move toward a great job. It's the knowledge that you are doing everything you can to make a good outcome.

If you're unemployed today, your confidence might be on thin ice. If you were recently laid off, or if you've been unemployed a long time, your confidence might be under water. It might take a leap of faith to think things will work out okay, but that's no reason not to get started. Some of the most accomplished candidates still feel nervous, especially when the stakes are high.

# The Inside Story

The first step toward a confident job interview is to remove the mystery surrounding employers and the interview process. For that, you need to know the inside story.

Interviewing candidates is harder than you think. Today, when the only real competitive edge a company has is the quality of its people and the productive team they become, the interviewer is supposed to determine whether you'd perform well in a job. In an hour, or a few hours at most, the interviewer tries to understand as much as possible about your skills, work experience, personality, personal and work-related values, stress tolerance, creativity, stamina, sense of humor . . . and on and on.

Most employers I know are good at locating candidates (and their resumes), but they wish they were more skilled at the very human—and very tricky—process of interviewing. Interviewers are under pressure to fill positions quickly. They're required to meet budgets (that means finding great people at the right price). They're expected to identify perfect candidates as well as "diamonds in the rough," and to be familiar with the details of many different types of jobs. Lurking in the background is the pressure not to hire the wrong person, which leads to business, morale, and sometimes even legal problems.

Interviewers are not doing you a favor by granting you an interview. Their jobs depend on making the right hires. In other words, their success depends on you!

As a candidate, you will talk to hiring managers, business owners, and others who were not trained as interviewers. Even though you cannot change the expertise of the person across the desk, you can improve the quality of your job interviews by knowing what the best interviewers are looking for. They want to know:

- Does this candidate have the skills to do the job?
- What results will the candidate produce consistently over time?
- How well does the candidate understand the job's goals, methods, and measures of success?

- How will this individual interact with other specific employees?
- What is this person's potential for growth?

Even if you aren't asked these questions directly, you must get this critical information across. That will make even an unskilled interviewer take notice!

## A Resume Is Not Enough

If a well-written resume were all it took to land a job, you'd be off the hook, but it isn't. Important as it is, a resume can only get you to the interview. It cannot close the sale for most jobs for the simple reason: factors that are often most crucial for success are hard to judge on paper.

Once you are face-to-face everything kicks into high gear. The interview is an *amazing* event—an attempt for both sides to predict the future while working through a maze of experiences and job requirements. It's unpredictable and complex, assessing both hard skills, like an ability to handle machinery, and soft skills, like having good judgment. It's a highly subjective, human event. Sometimes a person's interview feels fantastic but later their performance is lackluster. Sometimes the interview is awkward, but the person is hired and two years later they're a top performer.

To make things even more subjective, you're being compared not to the job description but to other candidates, and no two candidates are alike. The way to help an employer make the right decision—and thus hire you into the right job—is to become as clear and compelling as you can about the ways in which you have succeeded in the past.

## The Structure of a Job Interview

The typical interview has a simple four-part progression—first impressions and a brief discussion of the job requirements, a longer period discussing your qualifications, a chance for you to ask questions, and a closing period of open conversation. The interviewer is trying to get an accurate impression of you from all these different bits of information, and if you answer and ask questions well, the pieces of the puzzle come together to form a strong impression, like this:

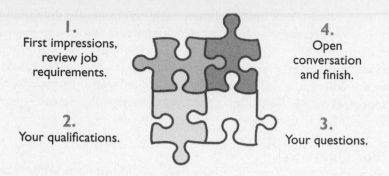

**1.**
First impressions, review job requirements.

**4.**
Open conversation and finish.

**2.**
Your qualifications.

**3.**
Your questions.

## First Impressions

First impressions set the tone. Your appearance is important, and just as important is your demeanor. Are you bright, active, and interesting? An interviewer is wondering, will I want the conversation to continue, or will I have to talk just long enough to be polite? There will be some small talk, and then you both dive in.

As you discuss the job requirements, most conversation naturally focuses on the actual tasks, activities, and goals of the job. Use this time to understand what defines success. Be alert for words like *outcome, results, expectations, goals, quota, target,* and *deadline* in the interviewer's questions—and use these criteria for success in your answers. This simple tactic helps you connect to the job in the interviewer's mind.

## Your Qualifications

Your qualifications are confirmed through a combination of reviewing your skills and experiences (usually by reviewing your resume) and telling stories of your work achievements. Your resume guides this part of the conversation; it takes up the longest part of the traditional interview. It's here you usually encounter that Monster moment when the interview tips toward getting the job . . . or not.

During the skills and experience review, you need to prove you have the exact skills required, or at least prove that you can acquire any missing skills quickly. Sometimes your potential to learn new skills will make your case. You also need to find out which of your skills might be in doubt, and be prepared to tell stories about the times you used those skills effectively.

Storytelling—your ability to share your experiences in the form of stories—is decisive. You have to relate details of how you overcame challenges similar enough to those in the new job. When you tell achievement stories, you might focus on the process you followed, on the skills you used, or on the results—usually your narrative contains all three. (These stories are so important that I've devoted chapter 6 entirely to them.)

## Your Questions

Interviewers often start the next phase of the interview with, "Any questions for me?" Questions you ask are absolutely critical to the long-term success of your job performance as well as your ability to land a job. Your questions prove your interest and commitment. Most candidates don't ask well-researched questions and lose this opportunity to prove they are better informed, more thoughtful, and more committed than the competition. (You'll learn how to ask great questions in chapter 11.)

## Open Conversation

Open conversation late in the interview either signals the closing of the interview or is an opportunity to dive deeper. The second is a sign that you are making a great impression. Now the interviewer is open to talk about how the company is doing against its competitors, or its plans for the future. Now talk about company culture and your own personal culture or work style usually comes up. Good interviewers respect someone who is choosing their next employer carefully, and most like to "sell" their companies to the candidate, if asked. (Remember, the interviewer is evaluating your fit for the entire interview, and might be using this time to confirm a general impression.)

Consistency through all four steps of the interview builds momentum. For example, if a key message for you is that you are a problem solver, you want to stress that ability throughout the interview by citing several examples of problems you've solved. You create an emotional atmosphere of confidence as well as a reason for the interviewer to dig deeper . . . and talk to you longer.

## Who Are You Talking To?

Interviewers aren't alike, and you will probably encounter several different types:

**Human Resources staff:** They are the first line of hiring for many companies. They cast a wide net, interviewing for many positions at many levels. They are highly effective interviewers. Employers with one hundred or more employees usually need a full-time HR person.

**Managers:** The hiring manager's focus is narrow—on the department and job in question. Not many managers, even in large corporations, are expert interviewers, but they have the ultimate decision to hire you. They also have clear expectations and detailed knowledge of the job, so dig deep with them to know if the job's right for you.

**Executives:** Executives focus on long-term business strategy, and they're particularly interested in assessing your growth potential. They have high standards, so if you've earned an interview with an executive, you're a serious candidate.

**Professional recruiters:** Headhunters locate and screen candidates for employers; they interview you with a specific position in mind. Their living depends on identifying great candidates quickly, so you can expect them to be skilled interviewers. They'll ask very specific questions about qualifications. Executive recruiters interview only for top-level positions.

Often you will not know the employer a recruiter represents until late in the process, so focus your preparation on an extrasharp presentation of your skills, experiences, and industry knowledge. Recruiters are better judges, and sharper critics, of a candidate's performance than typical line managers, so at the close of the interview, ask them how your presentation came off, and what you might improve.

## Interview Styles

Interviewers also have different personal styles. Here are six common types:

**The Inquisitor:** Never cracks a smile. Never diverts from a "show me" attitude. Fires off tough questions about your experience. The interviewer you imagine when you say, "I hate to interview." Your best reaction: Stay cool and project both respect and confidence. Don't think the tough, poker-faced attitude means you won't get the job. Often, the Inquisitor believes that a stressful interview unearths hidden qualities of a candidate. Often, the Inquisitor becomes your best advocate in the process and on into the job.

**The Buddy:** Smiles, jokes, tells you to relax. "Hey, let's go shoot some pool and talk about the job." There are actually two forms of Buddy I know: inept interviewers who just want to be liked, and expert interviewers who realize that setting you at ease can get you to reveal a lot of information you might otherwise not mention, like your salary range.

**The Laser Beam:** This interviewer focuses on one topic, such as a sales job's quota. Your strategy is to satisfy their judgment and move on. The Laser Beam is a common style for a line manager. Save your wide-ranging questions for the HR department.

**The Shotgun:** Fires questions all over the place. One minute you're talking about sales quotas and the next minute you're talking about company politics. The challenge is that the subjects don't seem connected, and you have no idea how they're making a judgment about you. This is where your careful presentation really pays off, because you can relate your strengths to many different aspects of the job.

**The Silver Bullet:** Believes there's one magic question to ask, and one magic answer that determines whether a candidate is right. The Silver Bullet asks a few perfunctory questions about your skills, then leans back and says, "Tell me, how do you tie your shoes?" or "If you could have dinner with three people, who would they be?" From your answer, the Silver Bullet decides yes or no. Answer simply . . . and move on.

**The Absentee:** Sometimes you'll meet an interviewer who's not mentally in the room. Maybe his boss dropped a big project on him earlier in the day, or maybe he's completely unprepared. It is almost impossible to make a strong impression on someone who is so distracted, so keep it simple. If they're time stressed, offer to reschedule the interview. Get your most important messages across and then focus more time on your follow-up.

You step into a position of power when you recognize the interviewer's style and format, and adjust your approach. As you read through the later chapters on interview methods and questions, ask, "How might my answers be different to match up with the interviewers?" With a Laser Beam type, you might offer them a choice when you begin your answer to a question ("Would you like to talk about this aspect of the job or that one?"). An achievement story for a Buddy might focus more on your teamwork skills, and the same story for an Inquisitor might begin by stating the results of your individual work. The more you show your "emotional intelligence" by understanding their objective for that interview, the more likely they will be to listen to you.

## Interview Formats

Within the general interview structure, you'll also find a number of different formats. The questions in chapters 3–9 of this book are organized according to interview formats, and you'll find detailed descriptions at the beginning of each chapter. Briefly, they are:

**Traditional interviews,** or the "freestyle" interview I described previously. Questions fall into the general groups of rapport building, skills and experience, education, and cultural matters.

**Storytelling interviews,** which revolve around detailed retellings of your work experiences.

**Management interviews,** which are focused on the particular concerns of management, such as your skills in hiring, motivating, and organizing teams.

**Stress interviews,** which test your mettle with a number of stress-inducing techniques. They're meant for high-stakes hiring.

**Special interview formats,** which you'll find in chapter 9, include variations on the traditional interview.

An interviewer (and in some cases, a group of interviewers collectively) can have three reactions to you, and only one will get you hired:

- "Each time I meet this person I like him or her more."
- "Each time I meet this person I like him or her less."
- "I don't know what to think of this person."

The candidate who thoughtfully steps into the place of the interviewer, and responds to their needs (not to a job description), will more likely receive that first reaction—and be closer to getting the job!

## What Were They Thinking?

A college graduate showed up for a job with his dad. When I met them, the father introduced himself and said he just wanted to make sure that he understood the job clearly, to help his son make the best decision. Then he offered to answer questions for his son!

I had to say that, unfortunately, only the job candidate could be in the interview. —*Marie Artim, Enterprise Rent-A-Car*

# EXERCISE

## Selling

Like it or not, a job interview is a sales call, and you are selling yourself. The candidate who has developed basic selling skills has a distinct advantage. Let's take a few methods from great sales representatives and relate them to your job interview—you can use one or more of these methods at any time in the interview.

*Sell value not price.* The interviewer, like any consumer, likes to feel that they're getting the most for their money. Selling value goes beyond proving you can do the job. It includes demonstrating your potential for growth, a strong work ethic, and those hard-to-quantify skills such as good judgment and creativity.

*Sell a solution.* Make sure you know the job's most important problem, such as raising the quality of a product, making customers happy, increasing some measure of productivity—and relate your skills directly to solving the problem.

*Sell outcomes.* Demonstrate your ability to produce the desired outcomes of the job, such as increased sales or a perfect safety record, by telling relevant achievement stories from past jobs.

*Sell skills.* A job opening by definition is a shortage of skills—there aren't enough people with the right skills at the organization. As part of selling solutions or outcomes, list the skills you have that produce outcomes critical to the job.

# SALES SHEET

*Sell value not price.* List three ways in which you are worth more than a candidate with similar experience and similar salary range. For example, describe how quickly you'll be able to take on additional responsibilities without requiring a promotion.

1. _____

2. _____

3. _____

*Sell a solution.* Write a real-world problem the employer faces and describe how you will solve it (citing research that mentions the problem makes this selling point much more powerful).

_____

_____

_____

*Sell outcomes.* List three desired outcomes of the job, and describe exactly how you will achieve them ... or better yet, how you have achieved them in the past.

1. _____
   _____

2. _____
   _____

3. _____
   _____

*Sell skills.* List the three top required skills and cite times you have used these skills well in a work setting. Quantify the results wherever possible.

1. _____
   _____

2. _____
   _____

3. _____
   _____

**You can download this form at monstercareers.com**

Joy finished writing her week's numbers on the calendar, then stepped back from the refrigerator. On Friday night, she and her husband Phil compared their activity for the week.

"Fourteen touches—fourteen points," she announced. "Three leads and two send-outs—ten points. One interview confirmed at Leffert Co.—three points. That's twenty-seven, plus ten for Wednesday's job interview . . . thirty-seven points!"

Phil wrote on the calendar as he spoke. "Ten touches—including six with existing customers, two new leads, two send-outs. One presentation, for ten points. That makes twenty-eight." Phil held Joy's hand in the air, crying "We have a winner!"

It was a game they played every Friday night since Joy began looking for a new position as a retail purchasing agent. Phil tracked his activity as a sales representative, and Joy recorded her job search activities. Quickly, Joy realized that only the most productive activities would win her enough points to beat Phil, and soon she looked forward to the week's scorekeeping.

"A good week," she declared. "I'll spend more time next week getting ready for the Leffert interview. They're looking for purchasing agents at two levels, so I have to figure out if I can shoot for the bigger job.

"Does this get any easier?" she asked, thinking of her limited time next week. "How do I know which touch is going to end up with an interview?"

"That's like asking which cast of the lure will catch the first fish," said Phil. "You just don't know, and that's why you write down your progress. But the interview shows you're doing a lot of things right."

Joy takes a lesson in good sales management from Phil: getting a job interview is partly a numbers game, and it helps to keep score. She tracks her weekly job search activity (using sales terms like touches, leads, and send-outs, which I'll explain below) and those numbers on the refrigerator tell her whether she's really making progress, or just filling her days with unproductive activity.

You have to work hard to land job interviews, and tracking your activity is one way to know that you're making progress. Sure, you might get lucky—find the perfect job, apply online, and interview two days later. That's a dream scenario, but don't trust your next job to luck. You have to build momentum day by day.

Momentum is a huge psychological boost in a job search. Once you locate your first job leads, you know you're on the right track. As you follow up with those leads, you learn more about the job market, and that turns into more leads. You learn to focus on the most productive activities, and ignore the distractions. You develop more options as new employers come to light. You no longer see yourself as a lonely figure casting into the darkness.

## Four Steps to Land an Interview

Proactive candidates—and I'll assume you're one of them—reach out to companies in a multistage approach:

- They briefly "touch" potential employers as a first contact.
- They capture "leads," the most promising prospects, with research and networking.
- They reach out to those leads with a "send-out," which tells the prospect more.
- They secure the "sales call," which for a candidate means getting the interview.

Let's apply these four steps to your job search.

## Touches

In this plan, a "touch" means a successful contact with a potential employer. It could be:

- First contact with a person at the employer (or a professional recruiter).
- Your approach to a hiring manager via networking, letter, e-mail, or a phone call.
- Applying online for a job you know you can do.
- First steps in networking; for example, calling a business acquaintance from several years ago.

Research feeds your touches by uncovering potential employers. At a minimum, you should study a prospective employer's Web site. If they don't have a Web site of their own—and even today, some smaller businesses don't—search the Web for a business directory listing or "storefront" such as those powered by Amazon or eBay.

As you research employers and jobs, take notes on the following:

- The name, location(s), and size of the company.
- The company's leadership: who they are and what they say about the business (usually found in the "About us" section of the Web site).
- What the company makes, or the services it provides.
- Who are the customers? (Other businesses? Consumers? Government?)
- What's the company's reputation—if they're large, what does the press say about them? Are they fast-moving, cautious, a leading company, or in the middle of the pack?
- What can you learn from a search on Google or Yahoo! Finance?

The quality of your touches is important. Tailor your touches with a cover letter or e-mail message that focuses on the issues your research has discovered. Solid, well-prepared touches require a little advance preparation. You need:

- A carefully written resume, the best one you can produce.
- A solid cover letter, describing who you are and what you're looking for.
- A strong understanding of the job(s) that are right for you.
- Some basic information about the employer—what they do, who their customers are, what their mission is—all easily found on the Internet or via networking.
- A practiced "sales pitch" describing your skills and qualifications.

Touches are a numbers game—the more touches, the more eventual interviews. Consider the numbers game of a typical job advertised online:

If 1,000 people read the job description, 100 may apply for the job. If you're one of them, you've just separated yourself from 900 others just by responding to the ad—but you're even more special, because your application is well prepared and you know you're qualified.

At this point, 10 candidates get an interview, including you. Now you're ahead of 990 of the original 1,000. You should feel pretty good about yourself—but recognize that the real competition starts here: 3 candidates get a second interview, and 1 candidate gets the job offer.

Don't stop sending out touches when you get a few leads! Even if you have a job interview scheduled, and have to focus for a couple of days on preparing for that interview, don't stop reaching out to other potential employers. If you get really active with your touches *and* keep their quality high, you will be amazed how many interviews you land in a short time.

Occasionally I hear about someone who's been looking for work for two years or more. My experience tells me that this person is typically quite stubborn in their initial touches. They blindly send out a hundred resumes and form letters—and nobody calls. Then they blindly send out another hundred resumes and again, nobody calls.

Alternatively, they focus relentlessly on only one or two employers, even after the employer has said "No, thanks" several times. At the same time, the candidate does little research, so they're unaware of possibilities that are right around the corner. If this is you, reinvent yourself. Start over, with a new resume, new target employers, a new suit, and a new attitude!

## Leads

If touches are one-way approaches, leads are two-way interactions, such as:

- A direct conversation with a decision maker, such as Human Resources staff or line managers at a target company.
- A response from a professional recruiter.
- A networking meeting that connects you to a specific employer.
- Developing a champion—a person at the employer who is interested enough in you to refer you to an employer.

It takes many touches to create a lead, so once you have one, don't let it slip away. Ask that person about their work and their organization. Find out exactly what they need to know to support you, and give it to them. You never know when they might become your champion—a few weeks later, a lunchroom conversation reminds them that their friend in the marketing department needs a new assistant. . . .

## Send-outs

Send-outs are the natural next step in the process. Someone has responded, so you send them more information. It could be someone with a specific job in mind, or it could be a face-to-face meeting with a networking contact (in that case, you're sending yourself out!). Examples of send-outs are:

- Sending a sample of your work, a written achievement story, or a testimonial from a former employer.
- Sending a second resume customized to highlight relevant accomplishments in your past.
- Sending requested resumes, work samples, etc.

- Setting up an informational interview with someone who can refer you to people who are hiring.
- Scheduling a networking meeting to discuss a specific job (but not with the hiring manager).

## Securing the Interview

At this point in the process, when you're in touch with an employer over a hot job lead, two things can happen: they get back in touch quickly . . . or they don't.

If they call or e-mail you right away, your next steps are simple. Get a date and time to meet. Ask a few strategic questions—request a job description if you haven't seen one yet, find out if you should prepare any materials in advance. Then prepare for the interview with the rest of this book!

When you make contact, be ready to discuss the job or your skills briefly, but don't talk for more than a minute or two. Don't detail your work experience, skills, or salary, or you may find you're having the interview right there, on the phone, and that's a mistake. You want to get face-to-face with the person who can hire you. It's just too easy for the person at the other end of a phone line to think, "Well, this one's not perfect, so I'll just keep looking." (Interviews for jobs in another state or country are an exception and I'll discuss those in chapter 9.)

Instead, respectfully insist on scheduling a meeting. "That's a really good question, Ms. Townsend, and I'd love to talk with you about it in person. I've scheduled next Wednesday and Friday for interviews. Which of those days is better for you?" Then . . . be quiet. The next person who talks loses the initiative.

What if the phone doesn't ring right away? Relax—most of the time it won't. Remember this is a numbers game, and a hundred factors you cannot control might stall the hiring process. Don't waste time fretting over events out of your control.

If a week or two passes when nothing happens to a once-hot job prospect, you may be in the place job seekers think of as the "black hole." Get out of the hole by generating more leads and send-outs around the job: Find people who work at the firm and can tell you more. Follow up by phone or e-mail directly to the person who will interview you.

Don't give up! As Calvin Coolidge said,

Nothing in the world can take the place of persistence. Talent will not; nothing is more common than unsuccessful men with talent. Genius will not; unrewarded genius is almost a proverb. Education will not; the world is full of educated derelicts. Persistence and determination alone are omnipotent. The slogan "Press On" has solved and always will solve the problems of the human race.

Having many irons in the fire helps break the silence: If you have two or three employers who have expressed interest, tell them that. Say, "I'm calling because I have two other job possibilities that are moving forward quickly, and I really want to make sure that I talk to you and learn more about the position (or your company) before I make a commitment to someone else."

Keep building momentum through touches, leads, send-outs, and follow-up! This creates movement toward success.

## My Best Advice

The more you know about what the interviewer is really looking for, and the implications of not filling that position, the more you can position your solution, which in the case of the interview is you. Otherwise, what you're doing is simply throwing out your personal "features and benefits" in the hope that some connect.

—Donald Weintraub, Rainmaker Associates

# When You Land an Interview

When you have an interview scheduled, it's time to double your research. You have to make the case that you will move the business toward its goals and for that, you need more information. Don't expect the interviewer to do this job for you. It's your effort to connect your strengths to their needs that powers a great interview.

You covered the basics in order to set up an appointment. Now find the answers to a few more focused questions:

- What is the business of the department, division, or group where you'd work? Do they make things, sell things, watch spending? Do they provide great customer service or manage operations? Find detailed answers.
- What is this specific job expected to accomplish?
- How do they measure success? I'm talking about actual numbers. Even in human-centered activities like customer service, performance can be measured. If you know how success is measured, you know what's really important in the job.
- Who would you work for? Who do they work for?

People within the organization can tell you a lot. Can you find them? A call to the HR department, saying you are doing research on the company before you apply for the job, is a respectable way to burrow inside a company. It's perfectly acceptable to ask some questions when setting up the interview, including:

- Who will I be talking to?
- Any suggestions on how to prepare?
- Should I expect a particular type of interview format?

When you can answer these questions, compare your resume and your research notes (including a job description or advertisement). Ask yourself, "What can I say about my skills and experience that will solve the job's problems or make the most of its opportunities? What work achievements in my past could be measured according to this job's standards for success?" Write down your answers; don't just imagine them. Actually writing them is the best way to know if they're legitimate.

## How to Practice

It's not only a matter of having good answers at the ready; practicing answers to common questions is critical to thinking the job through carefully.

You can't just wing it. You can't trust last-minute preparation (or luck) to perform well any more than you can pick up a guitar for the first time and play like a rock star. Use the following techniques to hone your performance:

- **Practice alone.** Imagine how you would answer the sample interview questions in chapters 3–9. Stand up and say your answers aloud, which is a great reality check. If you don't feel confident, go back to your resume, your research, or the Internet, and formulate an answer on paper according to the tactics in this book. Then rehearse that answer—standing up and speaking aloud.
- **Practice with a video camera.** Watching yourself on video can be incredibly helpful, as well as humbling. Face the camera as if it were the interviewer, and practice a 90-second sales pitch for yourself. Have a friend read questions and record the answers. Then watch the video, note where you can improve (especially in confidence-building habits like good eye contact, a smile, and projecting a positive attitude)—and practice again.
- **Practice with a partner or mentor.** A friend can ask questions you select from this book. He or she should note whether your answers are convincing, focused, and brief. Professional mentors, such as a former boss, are good at this. Their role of moving you along in your career is ideal for interview preparation.
- **Go to a mock interview.** A mock interview is a dress rehearsal with someone who is not actually interviewing you for a job, but otherwise it's staged exactly like a job interview. You make an appointment, dress correctly, and research the employer exactly

as if the mock interview were the real thing. A trained interviewer asks questions exactly like a genuine employer, and then gives you feedback on your performance. He or she is the career equivalent of a personal trainer! Colleges, career centers, and career coaches offer mock interviews (sometimes free to alumni).

Build interview practice into your job search routine; don't put it off until the last minute. Like all rehearsal, it's better to practice ten or twenty minutes every day than one hour the day before your performance.

## Study the Questions in this Book

Chapters 3–11 contain hundreds of interview questions, as well as discussions of each question's hidden meaning, and sample answers. The chapters are organized according to the type of questions that they answer. At the beginning of each chapter, you'll find a brief description and analysis of the type; for example, questions about your skills and experience, stressful questions, and questions for management candidates each have a separate chapter. You can read the chapters straight through or go to chapters that interest you right away.

Study both the questions and the interview strategies they reveal, and then, if you really want to be prepared, write down *your* answers to questions you may be asked. You can't be fully prepared just by reading—your practice for the interview should include going the extra mile to write detailed answers and practice them aloud.

If you do this, you will strengthen your own confidence. You will remember important details about your work experience. You'll feel much less intimidated by the interview process. And you'll send the right message, because real preparation proves you're ready to go the extra mile to land the job, and that's an attitude every interviewer likes to see.

## What Were They Thinking?

A candidate I know was asked, "Tell me about yourself," and the only thing she could think to say was, "I have a lot of shoes. I have my winter shoes and my summer shoes, and twice a year I switch them between the attic to the closet. I have pumps, and Manolo Blahniks, lots of different colors . . ." She went on and on. She just hadn't thought of the question before, and she drew a complete blank. All she could think about was her shoes.

Talk about not preparing! —Jeff Taylor

# EXERCISE

## Sales Score Sheet

Track your job search activity like a sales representative tracks his or her progress, suggests Monster sales executive Brian Graham. Brian's team sets aggressive goals for their work on a daily and weekly basis. Here are two methods for establishing a personal "score":

**The rule of four.** "At a very basic level, some sales representatives use the 'rule of four,'" explains Brian. "They give themselves one point for setting an appointment, one point for a meeting that has taken place, one point for any presentation or price quote, and so forth. If they get four points in a day, they've hit their goal. Five 4-point days in a row will fill your weekly schedule, guaranteed."

**The tracking game.** In the more advanced exercise, I've adapted the sales activity–tracking concept for your personal "sales" activity of landing job interviews. Using the "Touch-Lead-Send Out-Interview" sequence, you might set a goal of four touches a day, two leads a week, four or more send-outs a week, and three interviews a month.

The big advantage of this exercise is that you can see your progress day after day, and that is a huge motivating force. It also keeps you honest about how hard you're really looking for a job. If you have a friend or classmate who is also looking for work, compare scores at the end of each week. This can really get the competitive spirit going, as you encourage each other to beat your previous scores.

(Note: A quick reference chart describing touches, leads, send-outs, and interviews follows the sample score sheet.)

# SCORE SHEET

Touches get one point. Leads and send-outs get two points. Three points for setting a date for an interview. A completed job interview gets ten points.

**DATE:**

|  | Touches | Leads | Send-outs | Appointments | Interviews |
|---|---|---|---|---|---|
| Sunday |  |  |  |  |  |
| Monday |  |  |  |  |  |
| Tuesday |  |  |  |  |  |
| Wednesday |  |  |  |  |  |
| Thursday |  |  |  |  |  |
| Friday |  |  |  |  |  |
| Saturday |  |  |  |  |  |
| **Activity total** |  |  |  |  |  |
| Point Multiple | X1 | X2 | X2 | X3 | X10 |
| **Point Subtotal** |  |  |  |  |  |

**WEEKLY TOTAL SCORE:**

You can download this form at monstercareers.com.

# Reference for Score Sheet

| Touches: "Reaching out" | Leads: "Two-way conversations" | Send-outs: "Highly targeted and customized" | Securing the interview |
|---|---|---|---|
| • Research target companies.<br>• Post resume online.<br>• Apply for jobs online and offline.<br>• Do early networking. | • Talk with HR, line managers, and professional recruiters.<br>• Establish two-way contact with promising employers.<br>• Network toward a specific employer.<br>• Develop champions—people inside target organizations who will help. | • Send requested work samples or customized resume.<br>• Conduct an informational interview with person connected to employer.<br>• Have a networking meeting to discuss a specific job. | • Set a date and time.<br>• Ask questions to prepare for interview.<br>• Focus on intense pre-interview research. |

# EXERCISE

## Supercharged Selling Points

Executive recruiters, who operate where the stakes are very high, look for clues that you're a "high-octane" candidate. Whether or not you're going for an executive position, you can use these clues to boost your interview performance.

Write and then memorize details about any of the "talking points" below. Where appropriate, list them on your resume or in a cover letter. Be prepared to bring them into the conversation. These points go beyond what the average candidate has to offer . . . so don't be shy!

- Inside promotions—the people you worked for promoted you (as opposed to leaving jobs for promotions).
- Quantified results—percentage increases of revenue and cost savings, increased number of satisfied customers, etc.
- Reliable testimonials about your work achievements (beyond references, e.g., a fan letter from a customer).
- Clarity about where you want to go (a big indicator of success).
- Reputation in your field—speaking at events, being quoted in significant publications.
- Proven success—track record as an entrepreneur or problem fixer. (Tell this story in the Problem-Action-Result format described in chapter 6.)
- Connection with companies on the Fortune 500, Inc. 500, or other important list.
- A portfolio of successes, e.g., "trainer to the stars" or prestigious real estate sold.
- Information credited to you, e.g., patents, articles, white papers, etc.

T he HR people told you about the job, and your qualifications seem a pretty good fit," said Ron, the director of technology. "I have some questions of my own."

"Great," said Bob, who was eager to move into technical management. For a year he'd felt stuck in a rut at his current programming job, and he was excited to have this interview at SpruceNet, the hottest tech company in town. "I'm eager to tell you more, and to find out how you like to work."

Ron looked at Bob's resume. "Since I'd be your manager here, I'd like to know more about your likes and dislikes. Why don't you describe your best possible job?"

Bob had not expected this question so early, but replied without hesitation, "My best possible job would include daily programming tasks, with an emphasis on clean code, of course, but also leading a team on big-picture issues. For example, as we introduce a new feature on the Web site, how does it affect other areas? Have we tested the software thoroughly? How will the customers react?"

Ron interrupted. "Why is customer reaction to a new feature relevant?"

"Because," Bob replied, "I like getting results—not just any results, but the right ones. If the customers don't use the new feature, we've wasted our time, and worse, we're not building features that will improve the quality of the site. There's always a time/cost/quality trade-off with new features, so I establish those trade-offs up front. My *best possible job* would recognize this balancing act because otherwise we'd waste time correcting avoidable mistakes. I'd like to know if there is a strong quality assurance process here, but first, may I tell you about a time I managed that balancing act?"

"Go right ahead," said Ron.


Welcome to the question-and-answer chapters of *Monster Interviews.* The following chapters will show you how to take command of the interview by turning questions into conversations. As you will see, interview questions can be mastered by understanding the tactics that lie behind the question. Almost every interview question has dual purposes: first, to get factual information, and second, to evaluate intangible qualities (like confidence, judgment, and insight) that so often make the difference between success and failure in a job.

Different interview formats and styles reveal these intangible qualities, and for this reason, the chapters are organized according to interview formats. You'll also find two special situations that call for particular interview strategies in chapter 12.

The most common job interview format, which I call the "checklist" interview, is a matching game between your skills, experiences, and personality traits to a previously defined list. This is the interview you can count on having during your search. A typical interviewer then adds a few "freestyle" questions about culture, personality, and preferences.

Even at its best, the checklist interview has the feeling of a tennis game: the interviewer serves up a question and the candidate smacks it back. After an initial period of rapport building to set the candidate at ease, the interviewer asks some fact-finding questions (like "how did you find this opening?"), and then asks direct questions about skills, work experience, and work-related personal qualities. The resume and job description provide the framework of this interview.

You can take the checklist interview to a higher level of conversation. Great answers are based on facts that confirm your particular strengths. It's important that you do this consistently, because in a 1-hour interview, you might answer ten to twenty questions—ample time to give a consistently positive impression. In sports, business, and job interviews, consistency wins.

First, establish that you can do the job well, and then show your potential to go beyond the job description. As the interviewer becomes convinced that you can do the job (and that there are no "showstopper" negatives), he or she will seek to confirm this impression.

In this chapter, I'll explore the rapport-building and fact-finding part of the interview and describe answers to common questions asked during this phase. In chapter 4, you'll learn how to answer questions that explore your skills and work experience. In chapter 5, we'll cover the questions about education, culture, and personal fit that close this kind of interview.

## A Note About Question Format

**S**ample interview questions in this chapter and those that follow are formatted in four parts: the question, an analysis of the question's key points, a sample answer *(in italics)* based on a particular job and situation, and related questions. A few questions require only analysis and in those cases the sample answer does not appear.

## Rapport-Building Questions

In terms of making an impression, 20 percent of the interview takes place in the first few seconds. What's the energy when you come into a room? How do you say hello? Where do you sit? (There's no desk in my office, just a couch and three large chairs—which do you choose?) Do you sit right down, or stand nervously looking around, or wait for an invitation to sit?

The first rapport-building questions are usually big, fat, slow softballs. The inexperienced interviewer asks them to feel more comfortable. The experienced interviewer asks them to take your measure. Be alert! Sometimes you relax so much that you reveal things you don't want them to know. It can be an enjoyable beginning—why not hit that ball out of the park?

## What do you value most about your work?

Interviewers usually get clichés in answer to this question ("I really like the people."), or weak jokes ("Hey, it pays the rent."). I think this is an ideal time to make cultural connections. Is the company innovative? Talk about your love of innovation. Is it customer centered? Focus on how you've helped customers.

*I'm motivated by the chance to help people directly, and the great thing about customer service is that people come to me with a problem they've tried and failed to solve. Every day I get to make their lives better by solving that problem.*

**Related questions:**
- ▶ **What is the most satisfying thing about your job?**
- ▶ **Why would you stay in this job for a long time?**

## What interests do you have outside of work?

Show that you're an interesting person, not just a cog in the machine. Maybe you're a great weaver, so talk about the loom in your family room, and take out the scarf that you wove. You'll light up and show your enthusiasm—and have a chance to talk about how you'd translate that same energy to the job. There's no pressure here to be great at sports or arts and crafts, but there is some expectation that you do something interesting with your time outside of work.

*The reason I have put so much time into weaving is that I love detail. I love mastering hard skills, and I love creativity. Those are the qualities that I've come to love most in computer-assisted design . . . which is why I'm always trying to increase those skills.*

**Related questions:**
- ▶ **What do you do in your spare time?**
- ▶ **Do you have any hobbies?**
- ▶ **What do you like to do on weekends?**

## How would your spouse/best friend/closest relative describe you?

This tricky question diverts candidates into thinking about their relationships instead of the message they want to convey. Focus on one positive quality and put your answer in the context of work. (On rare occasions, this question might be used to determine your marital status. See chapter 10.)

*My spouse would tell you that I'm very conscientious at work, and would tell you about the time I dropped everything to take over for a sick coworker. He'd also say I'd warn him quickly if something happens that would make me late, so he's not caught by surprise at 6 P.M.*

**Related questions:**
- ▶ *What would your spouse/best friend/closest relative say is your most important quality?*
- ▶ *What would your spouse/best friend/closest relative say is your greatest strength/weakness?*

## What are you reading?

Mention recreational reading if this is asked lightly, and also note what you read to keep current with your work. Online reading counts, especially professional newsletters. If you see a book or other tip-off to the interviewer's outside interests, that's an opportunity to establish a common bond.

*For work, I just finished* Strategic Selling *and I'm curious to know if this department uses some of that book's sales techniques. To keep current, I get three online newsletters about sales management* [naming them]. *For recreation, I like intricate fiction like the books of Dan Brown or John Grisham. Oh and also . . .* [noticing a picture of the interviewer on a golf course] . . . *I devour every new issue of* Golf Digest. (But say this only if you actually do read the magazine!)

**Related questions:**
- ▶ *What was the last movie you enjoyed?*
- ▶ *What's your favorite film/book/TV show? (Hint: If you're like me—I read online all day but only two books a year—prepare well or you may not be able to remember the title or author!)*

## How about this lousy weather?

This is a toss-off question, but a poorly spoken candidate can turn it into a problem. Don't complain if you just hurt your back digging the car out of three feet of snow. Treat this question simply and be positive.

*Wow, I don't remember when we've had a week this stormy, but I'm glad we're getting some relief from last summer's drought. At least the lawns are happy.*

**Related question:**
▶ *Any remark about the weather, seasons, or ordinary events.*

## How about those Cardinals/Raiders/Titans/etc.?

Yes, there are some interviewers who will judge you on your interest in sports, or their other nonwork interests such as local news events, but most of the time this is a simple icebreaker. If you're a fan, enjoy the small talk; this alone can ease any nervousness you feel. If you don't follow the sport, don't fake it, but take the opportunity to show personal interest in the interviewer.

*How did they do last night? I haven't followed them closely this year . . . are you a fan?*

# Fact-finding Questions

Fact-finding questions might be asked at any time. Interviewers need to fill gaps in their knowledge about you to check off their list of "must haves," and quickly uncover signs of a bad fit. Fact-finding questions can tell you what information is most relevant to convey. Are most questions about your qualifications? They might have doubts whether you can do the job. Are more questions about what working conditions you require (salary, overtime, and environment)? In that case, they already think you can do the job but believe you might be unwilling to accept some of their conditions. When fact-finding questions come late in the interview, the interviewer is confirming or disproving his or her opinion.

## Tell me about your current job search.

Move beyond urgent ("I need a job today!") or lackadaisical ("I just thought I'd apply.") and show that your job search demonstrates good work habits. Be clear that you are looking for the right opportunity, not just any job. Show respect for the fact that you have competition for this job, whether they're interviewing one hundred candidates or just two.

*Despite the soft economy, it's an exciting time to be in the job market. I spent several weeks exploring opportunities for someone with my skills, and found some surprises [be prepared to cite examples]. I'm particularly interested in this position because of the chance to be with a smaller firm, where I feel I'll have more impact.*

**Related questions:**
- ▶ *Are you disappointed that there are so many candidates for this job? (Hint: Say no—you welcome the comparison to strong candidates.)*
- ▶ *This job would be a change for you. Tell me why you're looking for that. (Also see "Career Changers" on page 177.)*

## What kinds of opportunities are you looking for?

The interviewer wants to learn how much you have thought about your career. Are you looking for more money, or seeking to take on new challenges, or moving into management? Have you heard that ABC Company is a fun place to work? You should note the match between your skills and the job; employers are wary of candidates who talk at length about pursuing several types of jobs, which can indicate either indecision, a lack of commitment to the job, or even self-doubt.

*I decided to go into sales support a year ago so I could develop my ability to create profitable, long-term relationships. I can do that in only a limited way in my current position, and it's time to join a company where long-term customer relationships are a priority. That way, I can pursue my overall plan to move into sales full-time.*

**Related questions:**
- ▶ *Are you applying for other jobs at this company?*
- ▶ *Where do you hope this job will take you?*
- ▶ *What career options do you have at the moment?*

## Why do you want to work here?

This is similar to the previous question, but now the emphasis is "Why us and not our competition across town?" Do you care enough to research the differences among employers? What about this employer is both unique and relevant to your objectives?

*My research has shown that this company is an industry leader because of its constant innovation, and I also believe that's how you stay ahead. I read about your new service for customers on fixed incomes on your Web site, and it's similar to a service I helped create at my current employer. May I tell you about that?*

**Related questions:**
- ▶ *Why do you want this job?*
- ▶ *Why us and not XYZ company?*
- ▶ *Why a company that's so much smaller/bigger/faster than your current company?*

## What are your long-term objectives?

Strong candidates know where they're going, even if their plans might change in five years. Focus on the ways that this job is a step in a thoughtful path, and how your ambitions will benefit the employer. Stay away from answers that don't relate directly to the job such as your desire to move to the employer's regional area. That information is an "extra" that belongs later in the interview . . . when they're sold on you.

*I have loved to work with animals since I was young, and I hope someday to manage a training business. I believe the difference between a good trainer and a great one is often not how they work with pets, but how they work with pet owners. I know that your training method, with its emphasis on interaction and follow-up with owners as well as pets, will teach me the right ways to relate to all the various people who own animals.*

**Related questions:**
- ▶ *Tell me how this job fits into your career plan.*
- ▶ *Where do you see yourself five years from now? How do you plan to get there?*

# How did you hear about this position?

Emphasize why and how you're looking as well as where you found them. Are you passionate about the job or just shopping around? (Hint: Be passionate.) If they found your resume and called you, you can remind them, and still make that same positive statement. (Sometimes this question is asked to test the effectiveness of their job advertising.)

*I targeted this company two months ago, and connected with Phil Smith through a mutual friend. Phil and I had a great talk about your company, and confirmed you might have an opportunity in the production department this winter that closely matches my ideal job. I was really enthused by Phil's description of your "hands-on" expectations of employees; I have high expectations of my performance and hands-on is the best way to satisfy those expectations.*

**Related question:**
  ▶ *What methods are you using to locate job opportunities?*

# Where do you see yourself at this company in five years?

This can be a "gotcha" question: do you assume you'll still be working at the company in five years, or do you expect to move on? The disintegration of traditional loyalty between employers and employees has left managers just as shell-shocked as workers. This question can also be asked simply to measure your excitement about the organization, or your level of ambition.

*In five years I would expect to be working in a position of greater responsibility, based on my expectation of delivering more and more value as I acquire experience, make productive relationships with others, and take opportunities to distinguish my performance.*

**Related questions:**
  ▶ *The next step in this job is a management position. Make the case to me that you can grow into that position.*
  ▶ *Tell me how this job fits into your life plan.*

## What attracts you to this industry?

Passionate candidates learn about their industry as well as their job, and they are more likely to be satisfied as well as productive. Let your research show that you relate the job and the company to the big picture. Where is the industry going? What are its biggest challenges? Are you simply a worker or a member of a larger community?

*Fund-raising work is similar across many not-for-profit businesses and I've explored positions available in several areas, but I believe that the field of education is the critical place to be today. As a fund-raiser for your school, I'll have a direct, positive impact on the lives of young people, and I genuinely believe you're preparing leaders for the future. I've also found that when you represent education in fund-raising, you get very close to a wider variety of potential donors, and I like that variety.*

**Related questions:**
> ▶ **What do you most enjoy about this profession or industry?**
> ▶ **What led you to select this career path? What about this field interests you?**

## What do you know about us?

Your research of the company demonstrates your commitment and good work habits, as well as respect for the employer. Conversely, walking into an interview with no clue about the company's size, business, and news is insulting to the interviewer. Do you know what makes them different from their competition? Draw from all your sources: news items, financial performance, company culture, and positive comments from your network contacts (what you've heard directly from others is often more impressive than even Internet research). Then, focus on the benefit you would bring specific parts of the company and its business.

*Your current employees tell me exciting things about ABC Co., which I've confirmed with a visit to your Web site and other research. For example, your focus on making the best products in just three categories keeps you from getting into a price war with lower-quality manufacturers, and fits with my dedication to quality.*

**Related questions:**

▶ *Are you familiar with what we do here? From what you know so far, why would you be interested in working with us?*

▶ *Have you learned anything about this company since your application?*

▶ *Do you know what we do/what we make/which service we provide?*

▶ *What's the most important single quality of a person working here successfully?*

## My Best Advice

I sometimes ask questions that are completely irrelevant to the job, because they can show the difference between just listening and *active* listening. Maybe I ask, "Do you have an MBA?" when it's not in the job description. I could be asking for several reasons:

- I could have a positive association: I'm looking for an MBA because I see this as a growth position.
- I could have a negative association: in my last job, I might have seen terrible business decisions made by newly minted twenty-six-year-old MBAs.
- I might be looking for someone who shows a commitment to their education.
- My friend in another company might be looking for an MBA with your skills.

You don't know why I ask, and sometimes it doesn't matter whether you have that MBA. I want to know you're listening. Great candidates ask clarifying questions: "Is an MBA a requirement for the job? Tell me more about that. What skills do you see in MBAs that you're looking to find in the long term?" and so on. By asking those questions, you're showing that you're really interested in giving me what I'm looking for. You show your mind working.

*—Stephen Harper, Sanders Sales Institute*

## What do you consider to be this job's critical skills?

The main responsibilities are spelled out in the job description, so beyond quizzing your knowledge of the job, this question probes the match between the job's key tasks and your key strengths.

*First, a nurse must be technically competent, and we can discuss that in as much detail as you wish. My additional outstanding skills relate to the fact that a nurse is the key connection between patient and doctors: I communicate changes in a patient's condition rapidly and accurately; I recognize signs of more serious problems without supervision. My caring and attentive bedside manner gain the trust and cooperation of patients, which results in better treatment.*

**Related questions:**
- ▶ **What duties as a nurse [Web programmer, forklift operator, security officer, etc.] are key to success?**
- ▶ **What do you know about this job?**
- ▶ **What do you think this job's biggest challenge is?**
- ▶ **What is this job's main focus or goal?**

## What would you want to avoid in a new job?

Good employers also find out what candidates *don't* want in a job, and expect you to have opinions. Welcome the chance to tell them— but stay positive. Don't turn your answer into a list of demands, or you'll be spinning your way toward the door.

*I wish to avoid as much overnight travel as my current job requires. Fortunately, this job involves little travel.*

**Related question:**
- ▶ **Most people in this position complain about the long hours. Will the time demands be difficult for you to accept?**

## What do you least enjoy about your current or last job?

You mustn't fall into the trap of sounding negative, which is an interview killer. Be careful also of citing a job task that's key to the job you're discussing. There are two effective strategies for this question: cite a circumstance that is not a problem with the current job, and/or discuss a task you dislike that is much less a part of the job you're discussing.

*The least enjoyable part of my current job is that the company is doing very poorly, and I've had to lay off half my staff. I've done a good job, but the writing's clearly on the wall . . . that's why I'm here, after all.*

OR

*To be honest, I enjoyed the proofreading of print materials less and less as I took on more and more management of the marketing program. I'm glad to know that you have a full-time proofreader on staff so I can focus on the management tasks that are at the heart of this job.*

**Related questions:**
- ▶ **What don't you like about your current job?**
- ▶ **What have you outgrown, or become bored with, in your current work?**

## What are your salary expectations for this position?

Candidates rightly worry that if they name a salary that's too low, they'll be underpaid (or unjustly labeled "inexperienced") and if they name a figure that's too high, they'll price themselves out of the running. Don't talk about salary too early in the interview. You can postpone the discussion at least until they indicate you're a viable candidate by saying, "I'm sure this position pays a competitive salary, and I'll be happy to discuss that if you have come to the point where you'd like me to consider an offer."

When they're clearly interested and the time has come to put a few cards on the table, two tactics help:

First, know the market. Research salaries online. While this won't give you perfectly accurate information, it will be a good guide. Talk to people working in similar jobs or their managers to get some idea of what the job pays in your region of the country. When the time comes—often at the end of the interview—that you must discuss compensation, talk about as broad a range as you can. Include salary, benefits, and other compensation like bonuses, profit sharing, and stock options if they're available. Remind them that intangible job benefits, such as opportunity to grow, are just as important to you as money.

Second, always connect compensation to your unique ability to do the job. Remind the interviewer of the match between your skills and achievements and the job's requirements.

*I am sure that ABC Company pays a competitive salary. My research shows that here in Atlanta this position pays between $1,000 and $1,200 a week, and your Web site indicates you have strong benefits, including a possible performance bonus. I'm comfortable with that range, but let's make sure we are the right fit first!*

**Related questions:**
- ► *How much are you making in your current position?*
- ► *Do you have an idea of what this job pays?*
- ► *What's it going to take to get you to work here? (Also see "Aren't you overqualified . . . ?" on page 129.)*

## What is your salary history?

A different question from the one above, this is often asked as a setup tactic for later negotiation. If they know you accepted a 5 percent raise for your last two jobs, they'll calculate that you'll accept the same this time. Without refusing to answer, counter with your present market value: connect your answer to your research and overall job search. Again, if they insist, you will have to provide a history—but place your current salary expectations firmly in the present.

*My salary history demonstrates steady growth in every position I've held, as well as a clear direction for my career. This position—one I'm about to excel in—is a more responsible and valuable job than I have now. My research indicates that it is compensated in the range of $1,000 to $1,200 a week. That will bring my compensation, which has been lower in the past, to a fair value for my track record of high performance.*

**Related questions:**
- ► *Did you earn a bonus in your last position?*
- ► *What benefits have you received in the past?*

## What do you expect to get from this position in addition to salary and benefits?

Name the positives that are important to you, such as opportunity to learn and grow, technical challenges, cultural fit, prestige, and other factors. This is a chance to show your research and continue it with a well-placed question.

*First, this company is at the top of its game, and as someone who likes to win, I'm motivated by people who will challenge and beat the competition in every department, from sales to technical support. Second, I believe this position is highly visible to executive management, which is important to me. I'm not the anonymous-contributor type. Would you confirm that the spirit of doing better every year is part of the culture here, or is that just part of the sales department culture?*

**Related questions:**
▶ *We like to think of ourselves as a team. What do you get out of belonging to a team?*
▶ *Tell me how this job satisfies some ambition of yours that we haven't discussed.*

## Will you work overtime?

Questions about working conditions are qualifying questions: If asked early, it means the condition is required. If asked late in an interview, especially for a salaried position, you must probe further to know exactly what the expectations are. In either case, decide in advance what is acceptable and what is not.

*In my experience, there are some places where long hours are used only in a crisis, and others where it's part of the company culture. The key to a good decision, it seems to me, is clear expectations. Is overtime mandatory? Does this position pay extra for overtime? Will I be expected to come in on weekends? Will that be in crisis situations, or are employees expected to put in longer hours as a matter of course?*

**Related questions (all concerning working conditions):**
▶ *This job requires an all-out effort in the last week of every sales quarter. Would you have a problem making it a priority in those times?*
▶ *Describe your ideal amount of business travel.*
▶ *A twice-weekly shift at the loading dock is part of the job. Will you do it?*

▶ *The only slot we have available is the night shift. Is that acceptable?*

## Would you be willing to relocate?

This question should not come up for the first time in the job interview, but if it does, find out if relocation is required for the job under discussion or for advancement. Fewer than 50 percent of job seekers say they're willing to relocate for a new position, so if you are willing to move, that's a strong differentiator. (Incidentally, relocation help is frequently available for these positions. Ask details about compensation. A $60,000 salary goes a lot further in Tulsa than it does in Manhattan!)

*For the right opportunity, I'm open to relocating. Please tell me if frequent relocation is required for advancement at your firm.*

**Related questions:**
▶ *If we take you on, you must increase your professional grade by two levels in two years. You must do this on your own time. Is that okay?*
▶ *Will you split your time evenly between this branch office and the home office two hours' drive north of here?*

## What's the most important thing I need to know about you?

This question might come early or late in the interview. Answer it early, and you can go straight to your key messages; answer later, and you can repeat the critical job-landing criteria: the match, your skills, and your achievements.

*The most important thing you need to know about me is the close match between my history of achievements and this job's goals. That match should give you confidence that I can do the job well right away. It also proves that I'm ready to grow in this job, so you're fulfilling the job requirements today and investing in someone who will help the company grow in the coming years.*

**Related questions:**
- ▶ *If we had only one minute left in this interview, what would you tell me?*
- ▶ *What makes you different from other candidates?*

## Tell me about your work habits.

Which ones? Are they asking about time management, organizational skill, thoroughness? Often, this question is based on a bad experience with another employee. Name your personal strengths, and then ask for details.

*I'm disciplined about putting first things first. Work has a hundred distractions and blind alleys, so each day I list the priority work, then get it done before moving on to the B-level tasks. I know this habit has helped keep my time productive during this job search. I have high expectations of myself—and others—in terms of dependability, attention to detail, and keeping confidences. What habits do you think help guarantee this job's success?*

**Related questions:**
- ▶ *How do you decide what to do each day?*
- ▶ *Are you organized or disorganized?*

## What Were They Thinking?

One time, during the interviewing process, I had to tell a candidate that unfortunately we would not be able to offer him a job because, even if he qualified for the position, his drug test came back positive, and this was a drug/alcohol-free environment. He sadly said, "Oh, that's too bad." After thinking for a few minutes he looked up at me and said, "Can you tell me which one showed up on the test results?"
—*Anonymous Monster customer*

Lilies. Freesia. Tulips and irises everywhere. Roses of course—red, pink, white, and yellow. Outside the cold-storage cabinet, a row of bonsai trees. More for show than for sale, thought Jorge . . . they have no price tags. But they're real beauties.

Brian watched Jorge work on the arrangement, a late-spring basket for Mother's Day. "While you're doing that, tell me something: how do you make the customers remember you?" he asked.

"Well, you'll never beat the supermarket on price," said Jorge. "And everything you sell is a luxury . . . nobody's going to die if they don't get flowers. So I always get a little involved with their decisions—especially young people who don't know a thing about flowers. I ask them about the occasion, compliment their taste, and offer something unusual in their price range. People want to feel good about their luxuries, and if buying an arrangement is a more pleasurable experience than dropping six carnations on the checkout counter, they'll come back."

Nestling a white Siberian iris among the blues, Jorge tilted his head toward the briefcase on the counter. "I brought along a note from my favorite business customer back in New Jersey," he said. "Don't take my word for it—read what she had to say." He stepped back, drying his hands, and asked, "What do you think so far?"

Brian walked around the basket. "It's good." He thought to himself: so far, I think you're hired. "Let's see that note," he said.

Questions about your skills and work experience comprise the make-or-break phase of the interview. Skills are the best evidence you *can* do the job, and experience is the best evidence of *how well* you'll do the job.

Skills can be tested. Experience can be confirmed. These are solid pillars on which to set a hiring decision, which is why interviewers focus so much time on them.

In the example above, Brian tests Jorge's customer experience with questions at the same time he tests his ability to create a beautiful flower arrangement . . . because arranging flowers is only part of this job, and customer service is also critical.

Let's say you're interviewing for a training position. Early on, you'll say: I've been a trainer for X years (experience); I have coordinated training programs (skills); I have special presentation talents (skills). Make these points with an active voice: "Here are three examples of the training I've done over three years. Here are two books that I taught from—let me tell you how I used videoconferencing to save costs . . . and here's where I customized the program . . . and by the way, I know you asked for presentation skills. Let me tell you about my last presentation. . . ."

There are literally tens of thousands of skills used in the workplace; it's your job to find out in advance of the interview which are important to the job. If you're familiar with the required skills, you can discuss them as they relate to the job's goals. The job description or advertisement is your first line of information in finding out which skills are required. If you cannot get a job description in advance, you can learn a lot about required skills by talking to people in similar jobs.

And never, ever claim a skill you wouldn't be confident demonstrating right there in the interview. In the example above, Jorge created a unique flower arrangement before Brian's eyes, and his skill level was easy to judge. If you exaggerate your skills, you'll only give the interviewer ten minutes of amusement watching you fail the test . . . or a month of annoyance watching you fail in the job.

# General Skills Questions

## Tell me about your skills.

Focus on skills relevant to the job! First, check off the must-have skills. If they want to know more about specific skills, or nonwork skills, they'll ask. You'll lose their interest if you ramble on about your prowess in the kitchen (unless you're applying to be a chef).

*My top skills are a good fit with this executive assistant position: I am proficient in Microsoft Office and expert with Microsoft PowerPoint; I know how to juggle scheduling priorities and manage time to get the most important work done in a day. I treat people fairly and confidentially as they try to get time with executives, but I also know how to deflect time wasters. I can give you examples of all of these. May I show you two nonconfidential PowerPoint presentations I've created?*

**Related questions:**
▶ **Your cover letter says you have all the required skills for this job, but how good are you at each of them?**
▶ **What do you do best?**

## Which computer skills do you have?

If the job ad didn't specify which computer skills, ask the interviewer to specify. Indicate if your level of skill is higher than the job requires. You might talk about your home computer use in terms of learning "serious" software like financial-management packages. Don't mention nonbusiness activities like instant messaging or games—and be ready for a test.

*I can handle standard office productivity well, from spreadsheets to calendars to basic contact databases. I have a lot of practice with photo- and image-editing software from home, although I don't use that in my current position. Do you think that would be an additional asset in this job?*

**Related questions:**
▶ **How do you keep your e-mail organized?**

- ▶ *In your last position, how heavily did you use Excel [Access, QuickBooks, etc.]?*
- ▶ *This office runs on Macs. Are you comfortable with them?*

## What new skills would you like to gain from this position?

This question tests whether you've thought how the job advances your career. The skills you hope to learn must be relevant to the job's main responsibilities (not 10 percent of the job). New skills should increase your productivity. Although you can be flexible about long-term career goals, you should seek jobs that increase your value in the marketplace; employers respect that.

*I want to increase my ability to design Web sites that are easy to use. This firm's emphasis on quality testing means I would learn skills like designing and conducting usability tests quickly.*

**Related questions:**
- ▶ *How do you think this job will advance your career?*
- ▶ *Does this position really fit into your long-term plans?*

## Tell me about your special skills.

It's time to distinguish yourself, but it's not time to mention your expert poker game. Describe skills that enhance job performance, such as organizational or communication skills. Temperament-based skills, like an ability to stay focused in a fast-moving environment, also separate you from the pack.

*You've told me that this department, as a cost center, has to justify every penny it spends. Not only can I stick to a budget, but I have learned to measure the impact, in dollars, of my work on the sales side. Let me explain how. . . .*

**Related questions:**
- ▶ *Prove to me that you can go beyond the job description.*
- ▶ *Did your last position require tasks that this one does not?*

# How do you handle your current workload?

Anyone can say they work hard. The strong candidate uses this opportunity to prove they can accomplish important tasks while remaining flexible. Demands and priorities inevitably change—show you can handle that. In today's work environment, flexibility about time is an advantage, even in companies that stress work–life balance.

*Today, I get the important work done in about twenty hours a week—in fact I've outgrown the position and that's the reason I'm ready for a new challenge. The special projects I've taken on have been more demanding, sometimes requiring me to stay late or put in a few hours on weekends. . . . I manage my time carefully, understanding that emergencies call for flexibility.*

**Related questions:**
- ► *How do you set priorities in your work? What criteria do you use?*
- ► *Tell me about how you manage to accomplish so much in your current part-time position.*

# How do you know when your work is getting off-track? How do you get it back on track?

You don't need a certification from the Project Management Institute to show that you can correct mistakes. Managers value self-disciplined employees and dread high-maintenance staff. Give examples of times you saw work going wrong and corrected it, by either solving the problem or asking for appropriate help. Bonus points go to candidates who prove they had a backup plan in place when a project was upended by a sudden change.

*Planning begins with a deadline and a goal. Every day, I check the progress toward both, and if one is threatened, I alert my manager and staff. We make trade-offs based on the most important goals. I strive to act on small problems—such as a change in one team member's schedule—before they become big problems, and adjust accordingly.*

**Related questions:**
- ► *Tell me about a time you made an important self-correction at work.*

- ▶ *What are some of the things you do to work more efficiently?*
- ▶ *How do you manage long-term projects, and still get daily stuff done?*

## What kinds of problems did you handle day-to-day in your previous job? How did you go about solving them?

Show your judgment as well as your skill, and demonstrate you can solve problems without running to the boss for permission. Here's a real power answer: tell how you stopped a recurring problem by instituting a permanent change.

*One of the biggest annoyances for my last manager was chasing down staff to submit their expenses. I worked up a simpler expense form using Excel and then suggested something I learned in a previous job: that we repay on-time reports within forty-eight hours, but delay repayment of late expenses by sixty days. You'd be amazed how quickly that routine problem went away!*

**Related questions:**
- ▶ *How independent are you in solving the problems that every job has?*
- ▶ *What problems "ate time" for your last employer?*

## What types of problems do you enjoy solving?

Work problems are inevitable; problem-solving skills are uncommon. With this question, employers are probing not only whether you have those skills, but also your style. Do you spend time digging up the underlying causes of problems, or are you the knock-'em-down type of problem solver? Do you relish conflict or crave cooperation? Ask which approach is most valued at that workplace.

Whatever your style, you need to discuss strong problem-solving habits like facing a problem quickly, recording its details, and taking action. Can you deal with the unexpected? Can you de-escalate a serious problem? Do you take problems in stride or get flustered? A sure sign you're in the right profession is that you enjoy solving its difficulties.

*At the call center, you could say we do nothing but solve problems—for customers—but of course that's not the only business goal. In my current job, we spend a lot of time looking up information as well. I like the challenge of getting to the right information quickly, so we can solve the customer's problem in a cost-efficient manner. That's why I worked with three others to improve the problem-resolution files that the other CSRs used. . . .*

**Related questions:**
▶ **Do you consider yourself a problem solver? What kind?**
▶ **Would you say you spend more time cleaning up trouble, or more time preventing it from happening in the first place?**

## What do you do to keep yourself up-to-date with new technology?

Even if you're working in a nontechnical position, you can demonstrate curiosity and a desire to increase skills by knowing about the technical changes affecting your field. Be prepared with examples, and do your research on that specific company's technological challenges.

*I read two trade journals and subscribe to the leading industry newsletter. I also get a weekly e-mail alert from a general technology site, covering not only this business but also broader changes in technology, which is relevant to just about every job.*

**Related questions:**
▶ **Which technical changes are affecting this industry/ profession the most?**
▶ **Do you think the new XYZ technology would help you do this job better?**
▶ **Tell me about a technical problem that you solved in the last year, one for which you felt a great sense of accomplishment.**

## Do you speak any foreign languages?

Say more than "Sí." Define your level of verbal, listening, reading, and written language competency required for the position. Understand that your degree of fluency might decide your fitness for the job; a translator of legal documents needs a greater level of fluency than a receptionist. It is fine to ask which specific job activities will be conducted in languages other than English. And remember that the interviewer's next remark might be in another language!

*I am comfortable with conversational Spanish, and I can perform all the necessary tasks of this job in that language, including business correspondence. Would you like me to describe the features of this product in Spanish as if you were a potential customer?*

## How good a communicator are you?

How well you respond to this question will show how good you are. If you're confident of making a great impression, laugh and ask, "Well, how am I doing so far?" (Be prepared for a surprise answer, however.) Communication is so subjective that telling a story is the best way to convince the interviewer. Be as concrete as possible: this was the situation; here's how I communicated the information; this was the result. You also want some verification, so suggest one of your references who can honestly say you're a good communicator.

*The communication skill most important in my sales position is making my pitch relevant to the customer's long-term opportunities. Here's how I did that just last month with a potential customer. . . .*

If you have problems with communication, be candid. Although communication is increasingly important in business, lots of jobs are done well by silent people. If you aren't particularly articulate, tell how you have compensated for that and still achieved good business results.

*I'm not much of a public speaker, and fortunately that's not called for in this job. At the IT desk, it's been most important to listen to a caller and identify whether they can solve the problem themselves or whether I need to go over to their desk and help. I stay friendly, open, and helpful. Nontechnical people don't need complex explanations; they just need to get their problem solved.*

**Related questions:**
▶ **Pretend I am a friend who is going on a job interview tomorrow. How would you coach me to communicate effectively?**
▶ **What's the most important information to communicate in a crisis?**
▶ **What's your preferred way to tell your boss bad news?**

## How good are you with this equipment?

Whether you're talking about a digital blueprint plotter or a vending machine, your skill level is a key differentiator. Describe your technical skill first in any generally accepted industry benchmarks. ("I've been certified to level 4—expert—with this instrument.") If there are no independent benchmarks, give concrete examples of what you can do. Relate your technical skill to the big picture.

*There's a lot of data on this automobile diagnosis console, and I explain it carefully to the customer. I can operate it flawlessly every time, and I also give a little talk about what I'm doing, relating the advantages of a higher level of service. That gets the customer's car out of the bay in a timely manner and also demonstrates that he's getting a good deal—which means repeat business.*

**Related question:**
- ▶ **Okay, go ahead. (Not a question, but the "acid test" of operating the equipment during the job interview. Employers design tests that quickly verify a candidate's skill level with anything from a forklift to diagnostic software.)**

## What are the hallmarks of great customer service in any business?

"In any business" is an invitation to show you know the big picture—that customer service skills are critical to every job, including those in which the "customers" are other employees! Give concrete examples of how certain companies (the one you're interviewing with, I hope) listen to their customers, and change their products or practices based on what they learn. Discuss the importance of the "little things" like timeliness, respect, and genuine interest in the customers' comments.

*With so few technical barriers preventing a switch, customers stay loyal based on whom they trust, and who gives them respect as well as a good deal. I think this counts at all levels of the company, so perhaps you can tell me what people here who don't deal directly with customers do to enhance their experience.*

**Related questions:**
- ▶ *How does customer service affect your job's bottom-line results?*
- ▶ *What's most important to making your customers happy?*
- ▶ *Tell me about a time your work increased customer loyalty, even though they never knew about it directly.*

## How do you determine what your customers want?

First, define your customers. Everyone has them, even people who aren't making or selling products. If you're an executive assistant, for example, your customer is the executive *and* the people you schedule to meet with her.

Second, describe the need from the customer's point of view— what do they want, what will they pay for it, and what trade-offs will they make?

Finally, connect your actions directly to satisfying those needs. This goes a little beyond the question, but knowledge unconnected to action is useless in business.

*I pay a lot of attention to the information gathered by the customer service department, even though I'm in development. We meet monthly to talk about reactions to particular products and, in my capacity, I pay particular attention to how easy or hard it is to find a product on the Web site.*

**Related questions:**
- ▶ *What, other than a good price, can you offer a customer?*
- ▶ *How do you make customers so happy they'll pay a little more for your product?*

## My Best Advice

## Technical Skills

### Tell me about your technical skills.

Focus, focus, focus on the *relevant* technical skills. In many jobs these are a black-and-white issue: Can you operate this piece of equipment? Can you program in this language? Assuming you have the skill, the opportunity here is to prove your level of expertise and to differentiate yourself from the competition. You can do this by telling a story, by citing references ("My last boss will tell you that I'm an elegant Java programmer."), or by relating certifications ("I got my MCSE two years ago."). In the interview, probe the relative importance of the skill—if it's a skill you'll use daily, it's more important that you are able to do it without supervision.

Career changers, who often have skills irrelevant to the new job, tend to talk about their former expertise. Resist this backward-looking temptation, except to prove more general skills like being a fast learner of unfamiliar technologies.

*The job description and our talk today have focused on drafting. Is this a good time to show you some of the architectural renderings I brought in my portfolio? I can talk in detail about my CAD skills with these examples.*

**Related questions:**
▶ *How good are you at [skill]?*
▶ *What can a person who's more skilled in this job accomplish that a lesser-skilled person cannot?*

# How do you know your technical skills are a match for this job?

Stick to the facts, matching the job's required technical skills with your proven skills. Your answer can be as brief as a bulleted list.

*The job requires operating a Melbourne C400, and I've done that in my last job. This is an older model, which is why I suspect you've included maintenance skills in the job description. I kept a 10-year-old Melbourne running despite the fact that you can't get parts for it anymore. You also require a CME level 5 certification, which I got two years ago.*

**Related questions:**
- ▶ **Do you have proof of your skills?**
- ▶ **How do I know you're competent?**

# What are your strongest nonwork technical skills?

Even though this sounds like small talk, relate "irrelevant" skills to job performance. Show how your use of these skills displays valuable work habits, such as dedication, intelligence, attention to quality, or determination to finish goals.

*You can see from my resume that I'm passionate about music, and I've learned the best software package for composing fully orchestrated songs. Last year I composed a 30-minute musical accompaniment for my daughter's gymnastics recital; that took two months, working from 6 A.M. to 8 A.M., but the teachers, parents, and especially kids were delighted. I have that kind of passion when it comes to learning extras in page layout and production, because the technology's always changing, but the result has to be fabulous.*

**Related questions:**
- ▶ **Do you have skills that would equip you to grow in other parts of this business?**
- ▶ **Tell me something you do that's fun, but difficult.**

# How do you go about gathering information to solve a problem?

The interviewer is asking if you know the basics of research: Do you use multiple resources—Internet research, books, and journals—as well as ask the right people for expert help? Do you know which sources are reliable, or believe anything you read on an anonymous Internet blog? Leverage the research you did to prepare for the interview by describing it in detail.

*Before I applied for this job, I studied the company's Web site and did an Internet search for reliable news, but actually the richest sources of information about you came from the city newspaper's annual business roundup, as well as an informational interview I did with one of your employees.*

**Related questions:**
- ▶ **How do you gather data for important business decisions?**
- ▶ **When given a problem to solve, where do you start?**
- ▶ **How do you find your way through the tidal wave of information out there?**

## Sales Skills

### Tell me about your sales skills.

When it comes to sales skills, "Tell me" means "Sell me." There are many effective techniques used in sales; your task is to persuade the interviewer that your methods are appropriate to the job. If the interviewer is in sales, you can dive deep into jargon—"I think SPIN selling brings in the best relationship for this kind of client." If the interviewer is not in sales, keep the focus on your judgment and style, not terms they don't understand. Always close with a verification of your results.

*I've always been good at persuasion, which makes the approach fun, but clients are sophisticated these days and require a longer-term, solutions-oriented approach. I learned a lot from a mentor who used the strategic selling approach, and that's been a big part of my outstanding sales record—a 40-percent increase last year. Should we discuss how that approach applies to this job's clients?*

**Related questions:**
- ▶ **Tell me which selling skills you would use in this business development position.**

> ▶ **Describe how you would overcome a reluctance to pick up the phone and sell something.**
> ▶ **Tell me about winning back a customer who left.**
> ▶ **Who are your favorite customers?**

## When's the best time to close a sale?

Depending on the company, you may not "close" a sale at all. If you are a relationship-building style of sales manager, consider these points from Monster sales expert Vartan Hagopian:

*I don't "close" sales because the close is not a stand-alone event. I open business relationships and there is genuine dialogue with the customer continuously. This process leads to a natural solution where the customer is ready for the next step, which is implementation—and purchase happens during that time. The "close" is actually a process that begins at the opening of dialogue and continues throughout the relationship. When the close is difficult it usually means the process was cut short.*

**Related questions:**
> ▶ **What do you do with a prospect that cannot or will not decide to buy?**
> ▶ **Your competition took your best customer to lunch and really sold them well. Now the customer is threatening to break a contract. What do you do?**

## How do you respond to customers who say your product or service costs too much?

Interesting setup here: What if the interviewer concludes the interview by saying *you* cost too much? If you're in sales, you know the answer: ask questions to understand the budget issues; demonstrate creativity in negotiation, based on answering each party's interests; respond with a convincing summary of the value and benefits; and demonstrate that they're getting good value for the price, actually increasing revenue and saving money in the long run.

If you're not in sales . . . do the same!

*I ask questions about the total cost of the problem they're trying to solve.*

*I have demonstrated from the beginning of the conversation that my service or product is a great investment. The relationship constantly builds the case that "You get what you pay for."*

**Related questions:**

▶ **How do you get off a "yeah, but" cycle with the customer, in which they always return to price as the stumbling block?**

▶ **How do you prepare in advance for a customer who will try to bargain down your price?**

## Experience Questions

Experience is the second most important area of questioning in traditional interviews. Interviewers look for patterns in your past work that might help them predict how well you'll perform in the next job. You may relate past experiences to the next job, but don't make false comparisons. Spinning an irrelevant past experience into "proof" that you'll do the job well is spinning toward the door, not the job.

Even if interviewers say they've read your resume, review it with them. "That's great. I'd like to tell you more details about that project I mention in the second bullet point in my resume. . . ."

### Tell me about your work history.

Maybe they read your resume carefully, maybe not. You can't tell your entire work history in ninety seconds, so prepare a summary that relates the best of your work to the job in question. Also, position this job as a natural next step in a clearly thought out career progression.[1]

*Since earning my LISCW from the University of Illinois I've worked in three positions of increasing responsibility, one in a residential treatment center and two as an associate in private firms. I'll be happy to go into detail about my family therapy work in those positions. You'll also notice on*

---

[1] See chapters 7–9 of *Monster Careers: How to Land the Job of Your Life* for more about developing your 90-second "sales pitch."

*my resume that in all three jobs I've continued my studies, and acquired new skills—they're listed in bullets under the job descriptions—that are essential to this position, namely. . . .*

**Related questions:**
- ▶ **What's the most important point on this resume?**
- ▶ **Can you summarize your career for me?**
- ▶ **What has led you to this point in your career?**

## What special experience do you have that makes you right for this job?

Go beyond the job description. Tell how your particular experiences gave you greater insight, judgment, maturity, and skill. Structure your answer by making a big point, and back it up with a concrete experience.

*Many retail environments are stressful, and the person you hire should be able to smile through the chaos of the coming holiday season. I worked three holiday seasons during college in the Oak Tree gift shop in my hometown. That's the make-or-break season for that store, and I had the evening shift, when all the hassled, last-minute shoppers created absolute chaos. Let me tell you how I made them happy . . . and learned how a little extra attention resulted in extra sales.*

**Related questions:**
- ▶ **Does any experience in your work history stand out as unusual?**
- ▶ **You don't have quite as much experience as other candidates; why should I hire you?**
- ▶ **What in your previous job has prepared you for this position?**

## Give me an example of when you solved a problem by thinking "out of the box."

Often asked for creative positions, this question also sets up nicely for career changers, who need to argue that their untraditional background is a strength, not a weakness. Give detailed examples of creative problem solving: "It was always done like this . . . but I did it like that . . . for the following reasons . . . and got a superior result." If you know different problem-solving methods like brainstorming, future mapping, or "breakthrough" solutions, describe them.

*At XYZ Co., they lost a lot of money due to major equipment downtime. I was just the operations assistant, but I got the maintenance staff together for a brainstorming session and in two hours we came up with thirty low-cost ways to keep the machines running longer. I determined that the "hidden" problem was this: everyone was sticking to the maintenance schedule too rigidly. That kind of positive, questioning approach will be a strength in this project management job . . . and I still know how to follow a schedule!*

**Related questions:**
- ▶ **Tell me about a time when you came up with a creative idea and were able to use it or implement it at work. How did you do this?**
- ▶ **When is "the wrong approach" the right approach?**

## Tell me about your typical workday 6 A.M. to 6 P.M.

They're checking how you organize your time as well as your activities, and asking about a 12-hour day to get clues as to how you organize yourself outside of work. You don't have to give details for the full twelve hours, but show that you know what's most important, what's a distraction, and how you keep it all under control.

*I get in just after 8. After checking the associates' schedules, I'm on the floor by 8:30 for a quick look at the previous night's restocking. The next three hours are spent with the purchasers, with training, and I leave one hour for urgent e-mail or calls. Things get really busy in the afternoon, so I'm back on the floor. By 4 P.M. I'm back working long-term programs like hiring, bulk ordering, and physical plant.*

**Related questions:**
- ▶ **When do you like to arrive in the morning/leave at night?**
- ▶ **Are you a 40-hours-a-week type?**
- ▶ **How much of your day is routine, and how much is surprise?**

## What role did you play on that project?

Note that carefully chosen word, *role*, which means not only what you did, but what decision-making authority you had and where you fit into a team structure. Be precise about duties and mention outcomes of your work.

*As the project planner, my role was to make sure everyone had up-to-date schedules, including all the changes that took place the day before. Of course, that role also meant I would call everyone to check on their progress daily; I had to help people under deadline pressure keep their cool, make the changes that had to be made, and recommend critical trade-offs to the manager. Here's how I'd approach someone who slipped their deadline. . . .*

**Related questions:**
- ► **What can you take credit for in that project?**
- ► **Tell me about your level of responsibility in the XYZ program.**

## What were your primary roles and responsibilities at your previous job?

The facts are there on your resume. Use them as a springboard for the color commentary. Your answer should be very specific and focus on the skills that distinguish you from others. To avoid rambling, check in after a minute or so.

*Let me expand on my resume. As the associate dietitian at Whitman Hospital, I supervised the preparation and serving of menus planned by the chief dietitian. This required detailed record keeping, close planning with the outside food service, and ensuring promptness. Patients are already stressed, and meal service should be pleasant and predictable. I also participated in education and patient nutrition sessions. Would you like to know details of those?*

**Related questions:**
- ► **What did you do previously that nobody else was responsible for?**
- ► **What skills were indispensable at your previous job?**

## What did you like most about your previous job(s)? What were some of your best experiences?

Relate work experiences you enjoyed *because* they showed you at your best. The current position should offer similar opportunities. If the interviewer says, "Yes, you'll do that here, too," it's a sign they like you. Reminder: Don't exaggerate your accomplishments here; they can be easily checked against your resume. And don't tell them the best part of your last job was the annual holiday party, even if it was!

*My favorite activity was setting up a new recording installation—because every customer is different, every room is different, and there's nothing more satisfying than watching a customer say, "Wow, that sounds amazing." My skill at teaching customers what to listen for makes that possible. May I tell you about a particular challenge—setting up a studio in a carefully restored beach house?*

**Related questions:**
- ▶ **Tell me about a time you really felt good about your work.**
- ▶ **What motivates you in this job beyond money?**
- ▶ **What responsibilities do you miss most from your last job? What do you miss least?**

## In your current or last position, what are or were your five most significant accomplishments?

This question's a cinch—tell your best work achievement stories. If you don't have time to tell five achievements in detail, list them quickly, then ask which they'd like to hear in detail. (These five should appear on your resume.)

*I can tell you about my three biggest deals [name them] and two of my most significant contributions outside of the business development staff: the two excellent employees I recruited for my firm, and my help on the company's "good citizen" programs. Which would you like in detail?*

**Related questions:**
- ▶ **What proof do you have that you go "above and beyond" the job description?**
- ▶ **How have you distinguished yourself from your peers?**

## How have you helped to increase sales? Profits?

When they say "how," they mean "how much." Cite figures and specific examples whenever possible. For example, a help line representative increases customer satisfaction, which encourages sales. An assistant electrician helps increase sales by encouraging word-of-mouth advertising by every happy customer ("If you like us, tell a friend."). The "profits" part of this question gives you an easy close if you've ever saved money, because lower costs equal higher profits.

*Although I wasn't in the sales department, I talked to my manager frequently about our customers' priorities and found that on-time delivery was huge because it helped them plan their days. Without that, they bought our product in smaller quantities. So here's how my diligence improved on-time delivery by 20 percent. . . .*

**Related questions:**
- ▶ **This job is considered a cost center (non–revenue producing). How will you help our bottom line?**
- ▶ **How did your work contribute to the financial health of the company?**


## Have you helped reduce costs? How?

Prepare a detailed story in advance, telling how you delivered a service or product faster, more cheaply, or more reliably. If this is your first job, you can talk about how you saved money at home or for a school project.

*My sorority's fund-raising didn't quite come up to target for its activities last year, so I wrote up the budget and called a meeting where we first identified what we wanted to accomplish during the year, then brainstormed a combination of cutting some activities and finding cheaper alternatives for others.*

**Related questions:**
- ▶ **What do you do when it's clear your costs will be higher than anticipated?**
- ▶ **Tell me about a time you had to do more with less.**

## Tell me about working with clients or customers.

It's easy to say you love your customers but your behavior alone proves your attitude, so tell a great story describing how you exceeded client or customer expectations.

*The most valuable clients at our hotel's meeting center are the repeat customers. They want to get down to business, and for that reason, my staff and I should be nearly invisible. Of course the food, room setup, and service have to be good and I can tell you about those, but they also want flexibility. Six months ago, a group decided to add thirty guests at the last minute; the room wasn't big enough and all other rooms were booked. Let me tell you what I did to ensure that meeting came out great. . . .*

**Related questions:**
 ▶ *What do your clients want from you?*
 ▶ *What, from your client's or customer's point of view, is the difference between you and your competition?*

## What experience has been most important for your growth?

Growth as a person? Growth in your skills? Growth in your career? Stick with the third, and take this opportunity to show that you actively seek out growth.

*Even though my position was more than full-time, I volunteered to serve on the diversity task force for two reasons: it would help me understand this important issue facing every company, and frankly, it would give me a chance to show my intelligence and skills to some very important executives.*

**Related question:**
 ▶ *What have you done to "outgrow" your current job?*

## What has been your toughest job?

The interviewer will note carefully what you mean by "tough" here. You might safely go back several jobs if you can relate your story to the job for which you're interviewing. For example, this is a good opportunity for a candidate transitioning from military to civilian work, or for a career changer to show character, dedication, and good work habits.

*Well, candidly, the time I spent with my reserve unit in Iraq was the toughest job I'll ever do, and not only because of the physical danger, but because the stakes were so high. When other people's lives depend on the quality of your work, you learn to make a habit of double- and triple-checking everything. Let me tell you how I think that habit, under less stressful circumstances, will serve me and this company well in this position.*

**Related questions:**
- ▶ *Have you ever been in a job situation where you couldn't win?*
- ▶ *What are the greatest odds you have overcome in a job?*

## Describe your most difficult time at work.

Avoid the negativity trap—no blaming or complaining here. If you can, tell about a work problem common enough for the interviewer to have seen it before, or even to have been through it personally.

*My most difficult time? Definitely in the last six months, when I had to lay off 20 percent of my staff, and decide which people would be let go. If you've ever done that, you know it's a stressful time. Still, there are better and worse ways to help people transition from the company. Here's how I helped those people make a good exit, which shows my talent as a manager in tough times. . . .*

**Related question:**
- ▶ *Tell me about a time a work situation caused you great stress.*

## Describe a situation in which you had to arrive at a compromise.

The interviewer is not wondering if you make compromises, but how you make them . . . and probably comparing your style to the company's culture. Since that is hard to know in an interview, stick to a broad-minded answer. Tell how you sought to understand all sides of a conflict in the past. Did you take responsibility for pushing through a solution? Show you can be flexible and still get the job done.

*Last year we had a classic time-cost-quality problem with a product. As the person in charge of costs, I spied the problem early and went to the other team members, hammering out some cost savings and stripping away some unnecessary features. It was not easy to find lower-cost options, but we hit the deadline with a good product.*

**Related questions:**
- ▶ **What compromise could you make in this product/ service?**
- ▶ **Which features of this product are must-haves and which are just extras?**

## What Were They Thinking?

Recently we had a phone interview and face-to-face interview with someone we wanted to hire for a customer service position that would begin on May 15. Upon receiving the information from our background check, we found out that he would need a work visa to stay in the U.S., and our company does not provide that sponsorship. We told the candidate that we could not hire him without authorization to work in the U.S., and he responded, "I can get married by May 15!" He was dead serious.

—*Anonymous HR professional*

Rubin was a griller: he had asked tough questions for more than an hour, his pen never leaving his notepad. So Kim was surprised when he put the pen—a Waterman, she noticed, very expensive—behind his ear and shot her a quizzical smile.

"Hey," he said, "hey, I forgot to ask: what's your ideal job?"

Pause a moment, Kim told herself. Don't sound too rehearsed. She smiled back. Kim had shown off her business school smarts for two hours of interviews here at Brattle College; it was time to discuss what had led her to seek a university job after twelve years in management consulting.

"I'm glad you asked. Whew!" she blew out a breath in mock exhaustion. "This has been a great conversation, and I'm happy to tell you something very basic: I choose to work in a college environment because of my deep belief in the value of higher education. It's important in economic, intellectual, and yes, even spiritual growth. This job is an ideal next step as I apply my business skills to furthering the mission of this college."

"We get a lot of MBAs here who think they can hide out in academia," said Rubin. He slouched a little in his seat. "They think not-for-profit is less demanding than the real world."

"As you said a few minutes ago, Brattle College has to improve its standing in the academic community at large," Kim said. "Anybody looking for fewer demands than a for-profit environment shouldn't apply for this job . . . and you shouldn't hire them. You have a plan, and now you need measurable results year by year. May I tell you how I'd attack that as a business problem?"

"Let's talk about it at lunch with the provost," said Rubin.

. . .

Three topics in an interview offer you a chance to jump off the resume and jump into a richer conversation: education, personal and cultural fit, and closing remarks.

You might be asked about your education early or late in the interview. Whether you have a GED or a doctorate, your attitude toward learning new skills indicates how well you might perform in the job. Learning depends on specific knowledge and good habits, just like work, so it's an ideal analogy to how you'll perform in a job.

Questions about your values, preferences, and personal style—what I call personal culture—will be asked after the interviewer decides you have the skills and knowledge to do the job. These are important questions! When several candidates are qualified, personal culture can turn the decision.

Cultural questions, which usually comprise only a fraction of the interview, also offer great opportunities to sharpen the edges of your presentation. To the question about an ideal job above, Kim's easy answer could have been: "This one!" Rubin's response, of course, would have been, "Why?" and Kim would have been back at square one. Instead, Kim's more interesting answer described her ambitions, values, understanding of the job, and her deliberate career management.

Lastly, every interview ends with a couple of closing questions, and often candidates are so relieved to finish that they miss the opportunity to score a few late points. Pay careful attention to these closing minutes, because the last impression can be as powerful as the first. The interviewer is looking to confirm his or her opinion of you, and you are looking to keep the process spinning you toward the job!

# Education Questions

## In what ways do you feel that your education has prepared you for this job?

First, focus on the skills and knowledge you learned in school that are directly applicable to the job. Second, show that you *like* to use these skills, and enjoy increased proficiency. Third, comment on similarities between school and work.

*My degree in finance and my CPA demonstrate I have the required skills. Of these, forecasting is the most difficult and for me the most intriguing. I also feel that the workload at the University of Pennsylvania prepared me for the tight turnaround required for this job.*

**Related questions:**
- ▶ *Where did you learn your skills?*
- ▶ *Did you have this career in mind when you went to school?*

## What do you feel was your most important achievement in college?

Your choice of achievement says a lot about your work motivation. Did you set a goal to win a prestigious award? Were you driven to write the best thesis or create the best final project? Were you able to make the achievement a team effort?

*My most important achievement in college was designing and carrying out the lab work in crystal development. That required meticulous design, exacting attention to detail, and dedication (such as getting up at 2 A.M. to take measurements every night for three weeks). I wanted to take on a 6-month project like that because I was aiming for the Gould award for best science work . . . which I won!*

**Related question:**
- ▶ *Tell me about some schoolwork that made you proud.*

# How did you decide which college to attend?

Meaning, are you proud of your school? How are you deciding which employer to "attend"? Show that, even at age eighteen, you made decisions carefully. Wherever you went to school, discuss taking advantage of all the opportunities to grow. Talk about paying your own way through school, and use the opportunity to highlight a high grade point average.

*I did not believe that, at eighteen, I had to make a permanent decision between laying the foundation of a career in business and pursuing my interest in photography. That's why I applied to a number of colleges that had both strong business and arts programs. Of course, there was also a financial consideration, and in the end, Washington University in St. Louis fit all three beautifully.*

**Related questions:**
- ▶ **Where else do you wish you could have gone?**
- ▶ **If you could apply to school all over again, which ones would you pick?**

# Why do you have a GED and not a diploma?

This question might be asked aggressively, but a Graduate Equivalent Degree is nothing to be ashamed of. The hidden question is, "Did you leave school or drop out for a bad reason?" Explain the reason you left high school simply and directly—being evasive will kill your chances here—and then point out that getting your GED shows qualities that they want. You do not have to detail personal information (see chapter 10).

*I left school in the spring of 2004 for personal reasons, which are completely resolved now. I got my GED the following year because both my parents and I felt it was the right way to move on. I'm currently taking evening classes in business at Pioneer College. I have to be disciplined to get good grades and hold a part-time job, but that's the way to put my career on track. I plan to get my associate's degree in three years.*

**Related questions:**
- ▶ **Your grades indicate you barely scraped through school. What does that say about your performance in the future?**

▶ *I notice that, even though you matriculated at Cornell, you didn't complete four years there. Why's that?*

## How does your major apply to your career?

Translation: How do you make big decisions? Relate the process of deciding on a major to the process of forming your career ambitions. Are you just doing what comes easy, or are you pushing yourself forward? Even if your major is irrelevant to the position, you can demonstrate focus, determination, and the ability to learn quickly. You can demonstrate a deliberate decision-making process and a relevant range of interests.

*I took a variety of business courses in my senior year of high school, but it was the real-world experience of working in the back office of the Kennebec Inn that made me realize that hotel marketing management would allow me to combine my love of the hospitality business with my business skills. I chose Portland College because of its excellence in hospitality marketing.*

**Related questions:**
▶ **How did you decide on your major?**
▶ **How did you choose a topic for your honors thesis?**

## Tell me about your favorite professor in college.

Here, your professor is a proxy for your future boss, so make the connection plainly.

*My favorite professor was my thesis advisor, Sarah Blackman. She taught both my freshman and advanced chemistry courses. What I appreciated most was the way she managed her team of graduate students—who ran the lab work—to make sure everyone had a high level of technical skill from the get-go. I think that a good boss makes sure all team members have really solid foundations, because then there's no "weak player" to hold everyone back. Do you agree?*

**Related questions:**
▶ **Did you have a mentor in school? How did you work with him or her?**
▶ **What would your favorite professor say about you?**

# How have your internships prepared you to work here?

If you have used internships to gain work experience, good for you! Be highly specific as you draw on the similarities of your internship to the job at hand.

*This job requires succinct writing; two summers ago I wrote a catalog of XYZ Co.'s 125 training videos, and it was very important that the employees there find information quickly. So I also worked with one of the Web producers to put the catalog online, which made it much easier for people to choose the right training video for their staff.*

**Related question:**
▶ **Do you have any relevant work-study experience?**

# Are you continuing your education?

How ambitious are you? Will you work hard to increase your skills? Also, do you intend to leave us for graduate school in a few years? Is our tuition assistance program a plus for you? This question creates a number of follow-up issues. If you intend to continue your education, ask if that's valued at the employer. Your answer has to be concrete: "Well, sure, I'd like to . . . someday . . ." is meaningless.

*Yes. I never want to stop growing. If I were to come to work here, I would take advantage of tuition assistance for work-related study in the following areas. . . .*

**Related questions:**
▶ **Do you intend to go to graduate school?**
▶ **What additional training do you think you'll need in the next year?**
▶ **Are you interested in our tuition reimbursement program?**

# What did your education not prepare you for in this job?

This question, like the one above, tests whether you're a lifelong learner. The difference is, you'll fill gaps in your education on the job, not in night school. The interviewer is also wondering how self-aware you are, and whether you'll answer a hard question candidly.

*The emphasis at this company on managing toward the numbers— calculating return on investment even for people's time—was not part of my experience. I'm looking forward to learning that skill, because it will make me more effective.*

**Related questions:**
- ▶ **What in the world can a history major bring to a sales-driven company like ours?**
- ▶ **Describe the most important thing you want to learn in your first ninety days here.**

## What could you have done better in school?

Your answer reveals both self-awareness and personal performance standards, both closely watched by the interviewer.

*I'm pleased with my grades and academic performance. On reflection, I might have taken a few more courses outside my major area in order to be more conversant with broader issues. For example, there was an excellent course in cultural studies that might have prepared me more quickly for work with overseas clients. As it is, I've had to learn some of those cultural issues through my own study.*

**Related questions:**
- ▶ **Are you happy with your academic performance?**
- ▶ **We're thinking of going to your school for a recruiting visit—in what subjects would you say it's weakest?**

# Culture, Values, and Fit Questions

## Tell me about yourself.

This is the most open-ended question possible; often it's the first question of the interview. Connect to the job with a polished statement of your key qualifications. Their next question might be about one of those qualifications.

*The most important thing to know about me is that I love using my communication skills to help people. That is why I moved from selling to sales training. I'm good presenting to an audience, I know how to listen and ask questions when someone's having trouble, and I am particularly good at organizing training sessions around crowded schedules.*

## Thanks. And now tell me about you as a person.

Okay, they heard your speech and they'll get back to qualifications in a minute; now they want to know more. Think carefully about this answer: What makes you an interesting person? What's important to you? If you say, "I collect buttons and I watch a lot of TV," that doesn't tell me much. If you're really passionate about that button collection, if you want to talk about the history of buttons and the ways you use the Internet to find rare buttons, that's more interesting. This is a moment to show personal passion.

*My husband and I raise Guiding Eyes dogs. The organization entrusts one of its puppies to us for eighteen months and we take it through an intensive training program before it qualifies to work with blind people. We're on our third dog, a black Lab named Razzle. It's hard work—takes a lot of patience and time—but it's incredibly satisfying when your dog makes it, because only one out of ten does.*

## Tell me something about you I'd only know six months after you came to work here.

If you're building rapport with the interviewer, you could answer this with personal information ("I'm really funny; that's how I relieve stress, but you wouldn't know that today."). A short-and-sweet answer is "You'll know you made the right decision." A third strong answer relates a work habit to performance.

*Six months from now, you'll be surprised to learn how many people outside of my own department I've taken to lunch, asking them to describe their jobs and goals. I want to know this business from every angle.*

**Related questions:**
  ▶ *What hidden talents do you have?*
  ▶ *What skills do you have that you haven't used in a job? Would you use them here?*

## What results matter to you?

Are your goals and priorities the same as those of the business? Do you feel that your work has a positive impact, or do you think of yourself as a cog in a big machine?

*I succeed when the team hits its twin goals: a quality product delivered on time. Personally, my greatest satisfaction in my last job came when we delivered the lowest cost per thousand of parts in the HVAC line. I know my personal attention to cutting the actual paperwork without harming the quality-checking cycle made that possible.*

**Related questions:**
- ▶ **Are you more motivated by money or a job well done?**
- ▶ **How do you know an improvement at work was worth the effort?**

## Are you a lone wolf or a team player?

"They're trying to put you in a box with this question," observes Michael Neece, president of Interview Mastery. Don't step into that box. Jobs these days are highly interdependent, but also require the self-starting energy of the lone wolf. At the end of your reply, you can toss the cultural question back.

*It's hard to get meaningful work done in this field without teamwork. On a personal level, I've learned initiative is invaluable and I can tell you about a number of times I kept teams working together. I can also tell you about a time I had to just do the job myself. But help me apply my stories to this company—do you value teamwork above self-sufficiency?*

**Related questions:**
- ▶ **How do you get along with your coworkers at your current job?**
- ▶ **What makes teams effective?**
- ▶ **Would you prefer a position in which you had to accomplish everything yourself?**

## Do you work to live or live to work?

Okay, Candidate, which kind of extremist are you? This question is sometimes asked innocently enough but prompts doubts if you answer one or the other.

*I am passionately committed to the outcome of this work. True effectiveness isn't achieved by burning out on the job, however. My interests and activities outside of work feed my ability to get the job done. Is this company a "work hard/play hard" culture? Do people here make most of their friends through work?*

**Related questions:**
- ▶ **How seriously do you take your job?**
- ▶ **We all like to unwind. Can you leave your job here when you go home?**

## What motivates you?

A rote answer like "money" or "getting things done!" won't do here. Be specific. Describe a recent job situation that really got your energy flowing, and project that feeling forward into the new job. It's also strong to tell about a time you overcame a challenging situation or learned a new skill.

*Last July's storms brought down hundreds of trees, and even after the power was restored, our tree surgery demand tripled. As the Omaha branch office manager (no pun intended), I had to keep the trucks rolling, plan coverage for old customers and new, and still keep the crews working safe shifts. I was motivated by the chance to out-serve, out-respond, and outshine the competition. I changed our usual routine to keep up with demand, and learned some efficiencies, which we kept when business got back to normal.*

**Related questions:**
- ▶ **When have you felt completely committed to a project?**
- ▶ **What bores you?**
- ▶ **What gets you out of bed in the morning?**

## If money were no concern, what would you do?

Yes, there's a bit of a hidden agenda here: they'll remember your answer when it comes time to make you an offer. This isn't just a salary question, however. They want you to talk about interests, passions, and missions in your life. Why did you choose this job and this employer? It's safe to say, "Same work, more vacation," but maybe you would like to learn to play boogie piano, or build houses with Habitat for Humanity. The key is to show enthusiasm for the *work* first.

*If money were no concern, I would do this job on a dollar-a-year basis with an educational organization. As in this job, I'd design a better health curriculum, and put it online, and then I'd train the schools to use it regularly. That would combine my love of Web information design with a great need that I see in grammar schools today.*

**Related questions:**
- ▶ **How important is salary to your job satisfaction?**
- ▶ **If you could work anywhere, where would it be and why?**
- ▶ **What job has been most satisfying to you? Why?**
- ▶ **Describe your favorite work environment.**

## What is most important to you in a job?

Can the employer provide the environment where your motivation will kick in? Can they make the most of your talents? Beyond money, what do you care about—teamwork, flexible hours, public recognition, a chance to compete and win? Do you want to do one set of tasks or a wide variety? Be forthright about what's important to you and you'll both know whether you and the company are a good fit.

*I value a sense of progress and public accomplishment—candidly, I'm comfortable in the spotlight. This is a very visible position in one of your most valuable lines of business. The stakes are high, and I like to know my performance directly affects the company's bottom line.*

**Related questions:**
- ▶ **Describe the job of your dreams.**
- ▶ **What do you value most at work?**
- ▶ **If you could do only one part of this job, what would it be?**

## What's your work style?

Buttoned-down and quiet or loose and energetic? Intense or relaxed? You can't change your personality to suit a job and expect to succeed. If your research shows that your favorite style is also that of the company, you have a good fit. If you are unsure, show flexibility and a focus on the common goals of diverse work styles. Your answer can show self-awareness and confidence.

*My current employer and I are a good fit with work styles. I relate to management on a first-name basis, and I also know that a friendly, easygoing style with people can work with an uncompromising attitude toward hitting goals. That's why I like this company's way of keeping score with the bonus program your CEO described in last month's* Phoenix Business Journal.

**Related questions:**
- ▶ **What does "act professional" mean to you?**
- ▶ **Do you always wear that suit to work?**
- ▶ **How seriously do you take your job?**

## Describe your ideal job.

Saying "this one!" is fun, but doesn't move the conversation forward. While acknowledging the similarities between this job and your ideal, your answer should demonstrate insight into the job's goals and challenges.

*My ideal job would include daily programming tasks similar to this one, with an emphasis on immediate accuracy, of course, but also on big-picture issues. For example, as we introduce a new feature on the Web site, how does it affect other areas? Is there a strong quality assurance process in place? How will the customers react? The time/cost/quality trade-off is constant in computer engineering, and my track record shows I can really keep those trade-offs in mind from the beginning. My ideal job recognizes that balancing act.*

**Related questions:**
- ▶ **If money were not a factor, where would you like to work?**
- ▶ **What job has been most satisfying to you? Why?**
- ▶ **Describe your favorite work environment.**

## Tell me about the best boss you ever had.

Tell what you respect, as well as what you like. They might be thinking about your potential manager, or they might be listening carefully to know more about your values.

*I've been lucky enough to have good managers overall, and the one who really stands out was my first boss at XYZ Co. She combined high expectations for our performance with a lot of personal time developing our skills. Even though she had a big workload, she knew that by making us better, she could pass greater responsibility to us and everyone would grow.*

Related questions:
- ▶ *What was your favorite job in the past?*
- ▶ *Do you have a mentor? What is she or he like?*
- ▶ *Describe a really talented manager.*

## What company (or individual) is doing the best work in this field today?

Here's a chance to show you're intellectually on top of the business, because the deeper question is what criteria you use to pick the best—most profitable? Most mentions in *Fortune* magazine? Most admired? Then close with a good question about where the company sees itself. If you read business books, you might reference them.

*One of the best thinkers in the problems of customer management is Mary Smith, who published* The Awesome Art of Customer Management *last year. Have you read it? Let me tell you what I think her key, new insight is. . . .*

Related questions:
- ▶ *Which of our competitors do you admire?*
- ▶ *What do you think the next big thing in our business will be?*

## What makes you laugh?

Is this a serious question? Yes—but a tricky one. Your *attitude* toward the question is the test. Laugh in response, if you like, then relax and show some character in this rapport-building question. (Avoid controversy—racial, religious, or political humor, for example—but show insider knowledge if you can.)

*Pixar movies. Dave Barry. Your competition's claim to have a superior product.*

**Related questions:**
- ▶ ***What makes you cry, sing, and dance?***
- ▶ ***Any questions of personal taste: What's your favorite movie, favorite music, etc.?***

## How will you contribute to achieving this company's mission?

Hidden question: Have you bought into our mission? (You *did* read it on our Web site before you came in here, right?)

Relate the job or department goals to the overall mission. Point out that personal growth is important but secondary. If you've participated in developing a mission statement at work or elsewhere, tell about that. If you disagree with an employer's mission—you shouldn't be interviewing there.

*Big Box Co.'s mission is to help small-business travelers enjoy first-class travel accommodations. I like the fact that this company builds its business on making things better for the "little guy," because I've worked in small business myself. I know firsthand the frustrations of budget business travel.*

**Related questions:**
- ▶ ***What do you think of our mission?***
- ▶ ***Are mission statements just public relations, or are they real?***
- ▶ ***What does "mission" or "reason for existing" mean to you when it comes to a business?***

## How do you get along with different kinds of people?

This could relate to one of many specific situations: a difficult team setup, for example, or a company's diversity-recruiting efforts. For the former, tell about your successful teamwork. If they're clear it's the latter, you might ask how the company values diversity. Can you explain the benefits of a diverse workforce?[2] Can you listen to a variety

---

[2] You can learn more about this important topic at **diversity.monster.com**.

of viewpoints? If your experience to date is narrow, you might count the opportunity to work with different people a plus.

*When people of different temperaments come together, their different viewpoints can produce better results . . . if they all value teamwork and are focused on the same goals. Let me give you an example from my last job . . . [tell story].*

*A chance to work with a diversity of backgrounds and different points of view makes this job attractive to me. The audience for your services is growing and changing, and if we don't know the preferences of a number of customers, we'll fall behind.*

**Related questions:**
▶ *What efforts have you made to promote diversity in your company?*
▶ *Tell me about a time when you had to confront intolerant or ethnocentric behavior in the workplace.*

## Are you a leader or a follower?

Anyone can claim leadership; the confident candidate backs up the claim with multiple examples of success. Tell about a time you accomplished a goal that others in your position would not have accomplished. There are also times to let others lead, so tell about a time when you put personal glory aside for the sake of results.

*Over time, almost everyone has opportunities to lead and to follow, and knowing which role to play is a strength of mine; it comes down to not only job duties, but also what commitments I've made to a team, to my manager, and to myself. Would you like to know about a time I successfully led a group on my own initiative, or a time I decided that the most effective role for me was as a team member?*

**Related questions:**
▶ *What does "leadership" mean to you? (Hint: The employer's Web site may say what leadership means to them.)*
▶ *Give me an example of a time you had to give up a "starring role." Why did you do that?*

## How important is innovation to you?

How important is it to them? You'd better have studied their Web site, or networked with their employees, so you can judge whether a spirit of innovation is important to them. This question might be asked about many individual qualities, such as creativity, organization, and ambition. These qualities are important to the company *as long as they're aligned with the business goals.*

I like to say that "only the innovative thrive" in today's business environment, but innovation must be tied to performance.

*Innovation is the foundation of growth today, and as you'll see on my resume, I've proposed new ways of accomplishing our business goals. I also strongly believe that "Real artists ship products." Too often, companies lose focus because they mistake off-mission creativity with innovation.*

**Related questions:**
- ► **Do you think we should be satisfied with our current business?**
- ► **What would you change about this place in two years?**

## What's the most important thing we can teach our children?

This question is about values, not whether you have children (see chapter 10). You don't have to stick with business values, either, because this is also a chance to let a little more of your personal story out. Questions like these are often asked in third or fourth interviews, when they're 90 percent convinced you're right for the job.

*The Golden Rule. Responsibility. Accountability. We should teach children skills that will help them let go of the apron strings and become self-sufficient adults.*

**Related question:**
- ► **If you could name one quality everyone at this company should have, what would it be?**

### Has any big experience in your life changed your point of view about work?

It's your call whether you want to reveal personal information. Talk more about values than the actual experience. You may want to tell how the birth or adoption of a child made long hours at work seem less important. Or work may have seemed more important following a marriage or a child leaving for college. Stay away from politics, religion, and money matters, and negative events like divorce, if you can.

A less personal story about a big event is also perfectly appropriate. For example, many people found that after September 11, 2001, they wanted to rededicate themselves to family and community, as well as work.

*Two years ago, just before my father-in-law died, he asked us to give half his estate to charity. It was a shock* [laughing] *but the actual decisions about where his money would do the most good were among the most thoughtful of my life. It showed me that the monetary rewards of work could be greater than just buying a hot new car.*

**Related question:**
▶ **Describe a turning point in your career. What decisions did you make and why?**

## My Best Advice

Sometimes the interview just stalls. When that happens, ask one of these seven questions, any of which can refocus a lagging conversation:

- How do you see me helping you?
- What will you do if you can't find a candidate to fill this position?
- How long have you been dealing with this opening/issue/idea?
- What were you hoping I would say to you/show you today?
- I get the feeling you do/do not think I am a good fit. . . . Is that a fair statement?

- Can you help me understand your thinking?
- What about my resume/previous interview prompted our getting together today?

— Steve Harper, Sanders Sales Institute

## Closing Questions

You've gone through your resume, your education, and your skills and experience review. You built some rapport and discussed culture, and you sense the interview is coming to a close. Now, don't get too comfortable: hold your stature as a job seeker, as a candidate, because ultimately the rapport you developed at the beginning of the interview takes you confidently to the closing questions, which boil down to:

- "Where do we go from here?" or
- "Who else do I need to see to get this job?"

This is the time to repeat your key messages. Provide additional material such as work samples, letters of recommendation, and references. If you want the job, ask for it directly: "This looks like a good fit. If you agree, I want you to know that I'm enthusiastic about joining your team."

Pay attention to the buying signals. Are they telling you that they're interested? Are they beginning to sell you on the company? Talk briefly about next steps: Do they need anything else to help them make a decision? Do they know when they'll make a decision? Promise that you will call them within a week. (Then use the follow-up methods found in chapter 14.)

If they think you're right for the job, the interview might continue past your appointment time. This is a great sign! Resist the thought of saying, "Our scheduled time is over." The interview will come to its natural end, sometimes with an extended timeline in your favor.

## Is there anything else we need to know about you?

"No, that's it," is the wrong answer. You're a complete human being, and there's always something interesting to tell. Repeat your key messages, and then add one new point. You've answered the question and made your case.

*Yes! You want a personal trainer with three years' experience, and I have four. I hope my stories have convinced you that I'll make the members of the Middletown Health Club happy. We haven't yet discussed leadership, and while it's not in the job description, I think it's an important quality. You might have noticed that I was president of my sorority at Miami of Ohio, and I'd like to tell you how that leadership sets me apart from others.*

**Related questions:**
- ▶ **If there were one more thing you could tell me today, what would it be?**
- ▶ **What qualities make you right for the job, even if they're not in the job description?**
- ▶ **Tell me something unusual about yourself.**

## Based on what you now know about this position, how do you feel you would be able to contribute to the department you would be working for or the organization at large?

This is an invitation to reiterate what key business problem you'll solve, what key gaps your skills can fill, or why you're a good fit for the company. Show that you understand the job, the department, and the company.

*My skill at writing technical instructions will make other employees more effective, solve technical problems more quickly, and reduce calls to the help desk. All this gets back to making Aloe Solutions the "employer of choice" that's so important to the company . . . and to me!*

**Related questions:**
- ▶ **What's the most important contribution you can make?**
- ▶ **How well do you know this job's objectives?**

## Can you leave a list of references?

This is a very good sign! Reference checking is time-consuming, so if they ask for yours, it means you're a finalist for the job.

*Yes, I have two copies of my references here. Shall I tell them to expect your call?*

## If we were to offer you the job today, how soon could you start?

This question has a hidden edge: If you say you'll start tomorrow, you might look a little too eager to leave your current employer without warning, which is not professional behavior. If you ask for two months, they won't want to wait that long (occasional exception: senior executive positions). Plan an answer in advance of every interview, because dithering or making promises you can't keep ("I'll just cancel the family vacation.") leaves a negative impression.

If you are currently unemployed, ask for at least a few days to notify everyone that you've landed. If you have offers pending from several employers, be candid about your timing. Say, "I have one offer and I'm expecting another this week. If you made an offer today, I would tell that second company that I need to make a decision quickly."

Remember: A company that doesn't respect your giving a proper notice is suspect. Say, "I'm sure you want your employees to give ample notice so you'll understand that I must do the same at my current employer."

Finally, use this approach to ask about their timing:

*I'm convinced this is a great job, and it fits with my career plan overall. I feel a responsibility to give my current employer two weeks' notice, and then I would like to take five days off to close out my job search and clear my head for a weekend. If three weeks from today is acceptable, that would work for me. May I ask how soon you will make a decision?*

**Related questions:**
- ▶ **If you were presented with an offer, how soon would you be able to make a decision?**
- ▶ **We need someone in this position yesterday. Can you start tomorrow?**

## I have to check on salary requirements before we make a decision. How much do you need to make?

Your research should tell you roughly what the position pays, and you know what you need to make, so give a broad range (about 20 percent) in which you're comfortable. Postpone actual salary negotiations as long as possible.

*I have researched what this job pays in this area, and while salary is only one part of the decision, I would be comfortable in a range of $35,000 to $40,000, depending on benefits. Does this question mean you would like to offer me the job?*

**Related questions:**
- ▶ **I'm not sure this job pays as much as you're earning now—remind me how much your company pays for this?**
- ▶ **The salary is $35,000 per year. I hope that's okay?**

## Can you think of any reasons why you would not be able to perform this job?

There are at least two motivations for asking this question: First, the interviewer is giving you a chance to clear up any important doubts. Be honest with yourself and candid with them or you will set yourself up for failure. You can show confidence, and still get more information. Perhaps your doubts are unfounded.

*You have said that budget restrictions mean I could not add staff in the next year, yet your development plans call for a 12 percent increase in output. I don't believe that's a reason I would not be great for this job, but I wonder if you think it's a realistic goal?*

Second, this is an opening to discuss any concerns you have about accommodations for a disability. Under the Americans with Disabilities Act (ADA), a company must make "reasonable accommodations" to give disabled employees the same opportunities as nondisabled employees.

*I have a visual condition that prohibits driving but does not affect my ability to do the job. Shuttle bus service to this location is fine, but operates* only from 8 A.M. to 4:30 P.M.. Does that raise any concerns about "face time" in the office? Does anyone else in this company rely on the shuttle?

## What else do you need to know about us?

As a closing question, this is an invitation similar to the one above—are there any issues you need to close to decide you want the job? You may use this opportunity to show off your research by inquiring about a relevant development in their business, or you might ask a question related to the cultural fit between you and the company.

*Recently, you were named one of the ten best employers in the Twin Cities area. The reporter commented that this is a place where anyone can just walk into the boss's office for a chat. Now, senior managers are very busy, so . . . how does a junior-level person actually have a relationship with the big boss?*

**Related questions:**
- ▶ **What would you need to know to make a decision today to join us?**
- ▶ **Have you and I covered every important point?**

## What Were They Thinking?

As a new graduate, I managed to secure an interview with a CEO. Frankly, I was in way over my head. In the middle of the interview, the guy reached into his desk, pulled out a boat horn, and blasted it in my face. I was so intent on telling my story that I forced myself to ignore the outrageous behavior.
—*Dan Gregory, former president of Turnstone Press*

A fter the small talk, Judith came right to the point. "You wrote in your cover letter that you've earned a bigger job. Tell me about a time you exceeded expectations."

Mary silently thanked Judith, the comptroller of home products retailer RoomCo., for this perfect invitation to tell her best work story. Other interviewers, hearing that Mary was aiming for a big increase in responsibility in the sensitive area of finance, had put her on the defensive with their challenges to her background. Now she had a chance to overcome those doubts.

She began, "Although I am technically an 'assistant' financial analyst, let me tell you about my larger role in a big acquisition last year. I actually suggested the opportunity in the first place. When the business development team decided to explore the acquisition, I asked to do the financial analysis, and backed up the vice president in charge of those deals. When you hear the details, I'm sure you'll see that I've outgrown my current job, and why you'll want me on your team as RoomCo. carries on its expansion."

Human Resources professionals often structure an interview around work stories. Often called "behavior-based" interviewing, this method is based on the belief that your past behavior in job situations is the best predictor of your future behavior—for example, if you were highly responsive to customers in your last job, you'll be highly responsive to them in your next job.

The storytelling method also roots out clues about your hard-to-measure but critical qualities like ingenuity, leadership, or problem-solving style. For example, if you tell about a time you took on a new responsibility in a job, you'll describe how quickly you learn new skills, set priorities, and work with a manager, and how you relate your work to the company's big-picture mission. All this from a single real-world example!

It's hard to argue with a compelling narrative. Mary, above, believes she's stuck in her current job, and so she uses a strong story to prove not only that she's ready to take on more, but that she *has already* taken on more. If you can describe your accomplishments in detail, you can show that even gaps in your skills or experience can be overcome. Stories transform even a weak first impression into a strong lasting impression, and people remember narrative.

This style requires more preparation on your part. Write out stories of times you excelled, and memorize them. Use numbers wherever possible—increased sales, lowered costs, work done faster, customer complaints declined. Facts are highly persuasive. Draw from all your experience, and be mindful that recent work examples are most persuasive. You might use stories from life outside of work if they are highly relevant to the job being discussed.

A good achievement story starts with a statement of the problem you faced, moves quickly through the actions you took, and ends with the results of your work. It doesn't have to be long. Interview coach Carole Martin, author of *Boost Your Interview IQ*, gives this example of a story told by a candidate for a sales position:

**The Problem:** I had a customer who did not want to hear about the features of my merchandise because of a prior interaction with my company.

**The Action:** I listened to her story and made sure I heard her complaint. I then explained how I would have handled the situation differently and how I can offer her better service. I showed her some facts that changed her mind about dealing with the company again.

**The Result:** She not only bought the merchandise, but complimented me on how well I handled her account. She is now one of my best customers.

This story is brief, but is specific and has a happy outcome. The interviewer thinks, "I wish more of my sales team responded this way."

The storytelling format is especially helpful to entry-level candidates and career changers, who might not be able to cite experience in exactly the same line of work they wish to enter. By relating stories of other successes, these candidates can show important qualities like creative problem solving, perseverance, intelligence, and leadership.

Finally, telling a story makes you more interesting. Great speakers have always used stories to persuade their audiences and back up their claims, and like a public speaker, you have only a short time in which to make your points memorable.

Note: In the interests of space, the storytelling sample answers below in italics do not include a high level of detail. Instead, I've framed the most important issues and suggested ways to introduce your achievement stories.[3]

## My Best Advice

First and foremost: Practice a detailed presentation of your best accomplishments in advance. The biggest mistake I see candidates make is when I ask for a story and they look at me stunned, then grasp for the first story they can remember. It's usually not the best one . . . and I know they haven't prepared.

When telling the story, detail is compelling: How did the project start? How big was it? Were there challenging circumstances? Challenging individuals? What were the risks? What was the budget?

Now we're having a conversation, and that's better.

—*HR and recruiting consultant Ed Newman*

---

[3] There are detailed instructions for preparing these achievement stories on pages 127–130 of *Monster Careers: How to Land the Job of Your Life.*

# Storytelling Questions

### *Describe your most important work accomplishment.*

The accomplishment should be important to the employer, not just you. Show how you uncovered facts, balanced competing priorities, and used resources effectively. Did you use all available information to make decisions? Did you leave the most important decisions to someone else, or did you recommend solutions to your manager and defend them?

*Last summer I agreed to take over the reconstruction of an eight-mile bicycle path that had become a public embarrassment—broken signage, garbage everywhere, and neighbors complaining about teenage bonfire parties. Furthermore, the town had budgeted only $15,000 for this work, and early estimates said the job couldn't be done for less than $50,000.*

*Safety was clearly the bottom-line goal, but beyond that, the recreation department wanted to change its image from a cold bureaucracy to a caring community partner, so the first thing I did was spend 100 hours in meetings with neighbors, a town taxpayer group, and local conservation groups. We were all surprised by a hidden problem I uncovered. . . .*

**Related questions:**
- ▶ ***What proof can you offer that you can excel in this job?***
- ▶ ***Tell me about a job you did that made you proud.***

### *You said you're a problem solver. Give an example.*

Tell about solving a problem similar to one you'll encounter in the next job.

*In my current retail position, management supplied parts catalogs for the various departments, but these huge catalogs were regularly lost. One afternoon, I broke up a catalog by product lines. Then I bound these in laminated folders and hung each at the end of the appropriate aisle. Now associates can find unusual parts for customers quickly, instead of saying, "Uh, I don't know if we have that. . . ."*

**Related questions:**

▶ *Tell me about a time you identified a problem that had previously been overlooked.*

▶ *Tell me about a time you solved a really tough problem.*

## Give me an example of a time when you've taken the initiative.

The best story here is one in which the stakes were high—an urgent problem outside your formal responsibility that you solved anyway. They want to know that you're motivated by a chance to take action, and that your judgment is appropriate to the situation.

*Halfway through a big project it became clear that we were not going to make the deadline if we proceeded in the way we had planned. I brought the whole situation first to the team, and then took our recommendations to our manager. This is how I did that without undercutting the authority of others on the project . . . and got our work back on track. . . .*

**Related questions:**

▶ *Can you discuss a project in which you stepped outside your area of expertise?*

▶ *Tell me about a project you started on your own and what happened.*

▶ *Have you ever created a new process or a better way of doing your job?*

## Give me a situation that illustrates your ability to exercise good judgment.

To show your judgment, your story must walk the interviewer through the decision-making process: gathering unknown information; analyzing the situation from all angles; clearly weighing risks and trade-offs; and then coming to a definite decision. Of course, you should pick a story whose result shows your good judgment paid off.

*I took the opportunity of a team member's promotion to another department to reorganize my customer services staff. Although we were hitting our goals, I felt we could provide more valuable information to the sales department if we replaced the departing team member with someone who could collect and analyze consumer response data. Here's how I proceeded. . . .*

Related questions:
- ▶ **What's the best decision you ever made?**
- ▶ **Have you ever surprised a manager in a good way?**

## Tell me about the most difficult decision you ever had to make.

They're wondering *how* you made the decision, and also *why* it was difficult for you. These decisions are especially interesting (and memorable) if you show you considered the big picture. Were you aware of the effect of your decision on other people's lives? Were you consistent, fair, and practical? Did you act on your own or check your thinking with a mentor or peer? What were your personal and business goals? If you choose to tell about a personal decision, be careful to make it absolutely relevant to the job, as in this example:

*The decision to go back to school three years ago would be viewed by some as highly risky, and it was a complex decision. I had to put off buying a house, and step out of the workforce for two years. After careful analysis of what the degree meant to my long-term career plans, and making sure with my husband that we could handle student loans, we decided to make the investment in my career.*

Related questions:
- ▶ **Most decisions here are very complex. Give me an example of a challenging decision you had to make recently.**
- ▶ **I see on your resume you had to fire half your staff last year. Tell me about that.**

## Tell me about a time you disagreed with a decision your boss made.

Disagreement is inevitable; maturity is optional. So how did you handle it? Tell a story showing how you relate to a person who has greater decision-making authority than you. Did you still communicate well? Did you take it personally? Did you express your own point of view completely?

*The manager's neck is on the line when budget decisions are made. Last year I felt strongly that we should hire two additional staffers to cope with the work to which we had already committed, but my manager decided the money had to be spent on new technology. We discussed pros and cons, and I suggested ways to save enough to bring in one full-time freelancer, and then offered to find someone who was already skilled at the new technology. Even though I initially disagreed with her assessment, that solution worked out well all around.*

**Related questions:**
   ▶ *Every workplace has conflict—how do you handle it?*
   ▶ *How far will you go to defend your point of view?*
   ▶ *Let's say I disagree with the point you just made. Convince me.*
   ▶ *Tell me about a time you disagreed with the strategic direction of your department or company.*

### Tell me the story of your hardest assignment.

Another great opportunity—if you're prepared! Choose a story with a good outcome, and be specific in what you mean by "hardest." Show how you grew by facing a real challenge.

*It was clear that customers were less loyal than they had been in the past, and my sales job was reduced to "saving" sales instead of making big new ones. This is a crisis for a sales manager—in a few months, you fall too far behind. So I delegated most office tasks and went on a series of twenty face-to-face calls in sixty days. Here's how I did it, how I grew sales and, for that matter, how I got back to the essential customer relationship skills that had gotten a little rusty since I became a manager. . . .*

**Related questions:**
   ▶ *Can you describe your hardest achievement outside of work?*
   ▶ *We all have times we're given an "impossible" task. What did you do when that happened to you?*

▶ **Tell me about a time you went beyond the job description.**

## Tell me about your skills in [relevant field].

From accounting to zoology, every field requires special skills, knowledge, and methods. Prepare to discuss must-have skills and find out ought-to-haves. Refer directly to the job description. Show that you understand the job's priorities and the larger context.

*Let me confirm the most important skills in this job* [list them]. *Okay, clearly the bottom line for a paralegal at your firm is the thoroughness of the research, and the ability to draft reports quickly. I'll tell you about a very tough research project last year that I completed under a tight deadline.*

**Related questions:**
▶ **Can you prove you're better at [skill] than other candidates?**
▶ **You've had this skill for only a year. How do I know you're strong in it?**

## Additional Storytelling Questions

## Tell me about the best team that you've worked on.

Your story should demonstrate how success came from good teamwork, and then, how your contribution made the team successful. Give details about your role, your authority, and your interactions with team members. Teamwork means working toward a common goal, good communication, clear responsibilities, and clear decision-making processes. Tell about a time you gave a team credit, not just yourself.

**Related questions:**
▶ **What do you see as the advantages to working in a team environment?**
▶ **How do you use teamwork to be more effective?**

**Tell me about a time when your project looked as if it was not going to hit a deadline.**

"Hit a deadline" also means "keep your promises." Tell about keeping a commitment through effective planning, anticipating problems, and good project management. Tell how you knew the deadline was in jeopardy, and what actions you took to bring the project back on track, especially if managing other people. Tell what lessons you learned and how you'll apply them to the next project.

**Related questions:**
▶ *Give me an example of a time something went wrong on a project.*
▶ *How do I know you'll go the extra mile to hit this job's goals?*

**Tell me about a time you finished a job early or under-budget.**

What a great opportunity to shine! Be specific about your impact on a successful project. Tell what you did with the time and cost savings—expand the original goal? Begin an extra project? You might tell your story strategically to imply that you are ready for more challenging work. (Incidentally, this is a great story to prepare for performance review interviews at your current place of work.)

**Related questions:**
▶ *Tell me about a success.*
▶ *Ever have a project go so well you expanded its original scope?*

**Tell me about a time you came up with a creative solution to a problem.**

If you work in a creative field such as advertising, this is the time to pull out your portfolio and describe the process of your work. If you are in another field, tell about a time when solving a problem in an innovative way was your idea (not someone else's idea).

**Related questions:**
- ▶ *Everyone talks about innovation here. Prove you can innovate.*
- ▶ *Tell me what separates you from people who have exactly the same skills.*

## What Were They Thinking?

This story was told to me by a recruiter at a major restaurant corporation, who was interviewing a candidate to manage a restaurant.

*Recruiter:* "Tell me about a time you and your boss had a disagreement."

*Candidate:* "Oh, sure. I was working in a bar, and someone took $80 from the cash register. It wasn't me! Anyway, the boss thought it was me, so he put my fingers in the cash register drawer and slammed it over and over. Look—you can still see the scars!"

"How do you motivate your staff?" asked Jill.

Karen replied, "I motivate individuals on my staff according to their temperaments and personal priorities. One is highly motivated by tackling new challenges, one needs a lot of public praise, and one loves his job because while I'm demanding about results, I also am flexible about personal schedules. Money is a motivator, so I set measurable, objective goals for everyone to earn a bonus. . . ."

Karen paused, considering whether to launch into a story, and then decided to state a key message first. "I will tell you about a time I motivated a team of five managers to exceed their department's goals, but before I do, consider this: Motivation begins with hiring. Management's job is to hire self-starters and clear the path for them to do their best work. Would you like to know more about how I hire self-motivated people?"

As a candidate for senior management, Karen answers Jill's questions with detailed stories, and also positions herself as a leader, not just someone who can do the job.

Management interviews dig deep into how someone motivates, directs, and disciplines others to achieve business goals. They focus first on results, which is why you must have well-practiced achievements to discuss in detail. They also test whether you see the big picture—how all the moving components and separate agendas of a company interact. Finally, there is more emphasis on personal and company culture in this interview, because management's success is intimately tied to both.

Karen's answer shows her broad experience: She first speaks plainly about how to motivate staff, offers a story, and then adds her belief that motivation starts with the hiring process. She'll go on to discuss her strong hiring record, which opens up the conversation to her strengths.

They want someone who can take the organization further. Your goal as a management candidate is to show how far you can go. More than other candidates, managers are expected to pursue growth and learning. You should know the competition more fully. You should demonstrate that you have thought long and carefully about your abilities, management style, and career path. After all, if you get that job, you'll be the boss!

## Management Interview Questions and Answers

### Tell me about one of the most important business problems you ever faced.

Your choice of the problem described is critical. It must be strategic, to show you can handle the make-or-break issues facing a company. Tell how the problem affected the business as a whole, and how you understood not just the symptoms of the problem but all the underlying issues. Show how your actions demonstrated leadership, thoroughness, or other qualities needed in the new job. And finally, state the (good) outcome!

*Our Web e-commerce platform was so difficult to use it cost the company an estimated $4.6 million in lost sales. There were three global benefits to installing a new system: greater revenue from new customers, greater revenue from reducing abandonment rates from existing customers, and much lower customer support and training costs. I can show you the presentation I gave* *to senior management that got the go-ahead to examine new e-commerce technologies, but first let me tell you how I pulled together an ad hoc team from all over the company to make a solid analysis of the problem and opportunity. . . .*

**Related questions:**
- ▶ **What's your biggest win at your current job?**
- ▶ **How do you get senior management to tackle a big problem?**
- ▶ **Have you ever seized a big opportunity? What happened?**

## What is your favorite management style?

Does your style conform to the company's culture? If not, can you make the case for change? Given that different styles can achieve the same results, why do you choose one over the other? Have you really thought through your style, or do you manage by gut feel? Do you know your strengths and weaknesses? Describe your style quickly, and then give an example of why—and where—this style delivers superior results. Your answer is important to the long-term fit both you and the interviewer seek.

*I manage my people by setting clear expectations for both performance and behavior. As a client-based business, we rely on good communication and a professional demeanor, so I end up coaching my eight direct reports in those qualities. If I solve every problem myself, staff doesn't grow and I don't have time to focus on strategic issues like client development. I am not a micromanager so I hired a second-in-command who is very strong in process detail. Finally, I try to set an example of maintaining some work–life balance. It's hard to find good people, and burning them out is harmful in the long run.*

**Related questions:**
- ▶ **Do you lead by example, by demand, or by setting a vision?**
- ▶ **Describe the style of the best boss you ever had.**
- ▶ **Tell me about a time you changed your style to suit a situation.**

## Tell me why and how you would fire someone.

*Why* and *how* are two different questions—and that's the point of asking the question this way.

*Why:* What are your bottom-line reasons to fire someone? Does your answer reveal subtle prejudices ("the older guy just didn't fit in"), or is it based on objective criteria? Do you dodge responsibility by citing layoffs or orders from above, or do you assume responsibility for a difficult task?

*How:* Whatever the reason for firing, they're looking for a process that's fair, legal, and good for the business in the long run. If you have a clear-cut story ("I fired him for cheating customers."), you have an easy answer. If you fired an underachiever, list the steps you took to give him a fair chance to save his job. Don't name an individual but keep your answer on an objective level.

*I don't know any manager who likes to fire people, but if someone's in the wrong position it's not healthy for him or the company. The process I went through included performance assessment, coaching, a "probationary" period with clear goals to hit, and then an exit from the company. I sought help from HR all the way, and they helped me make certain the employee got a fair shake. Let me tell you how I knew the individual was underperforming, and how I determined she would become a drag on the team, never reach her own potential, and hurt the company's reputation. . . .*

**Related questions:**
- ▶ **Tell me about a time when you had to confront someone who had failed in their job.**
- ▶ **If layoffs force you to lose 20 percent of your staff, how do you choose whom to fire?**
- ▶ **Describe a reason you'd fire someone instantly, with no second chances.**

## Tell me why and how you would hire someone.

Strong hiring makes all the difference, and strong managers follow a disciplined process. Weak managers hire by "gut feel" and hope they're lucky. Talk about how you found your best performers, screened their talents, and put them through their paces in a job interview. Display your knowledge of the long-term grooming of employees. Did someone you hired go on to do great things? Say so.

*The "why" is easy: to create a new opportunity and fill gaps in my current team's performance. The "how" takes a little longer, because I am very selective. I believe it's better to keep looking rather than settle on a candidate who is, say, 80 percent of what I want. Let me tell you about a career changer I brought into my department, someone who was different from other candidates, and how I identified the qualities that would make him a leader, and the spectacular results we're seeing after four months. . . .*

**Related questions:**
- ▶ *What's most important in hiring: speed or quality?*
- ▶ *Tell me about a time when you paid more for a candidate than was budgeted.*
- ▶ *How have you expanded your team? What direction did you set and how did you achieve that?*

### How do you get the most out of a team?

What do they mean by "the most"—making a team more efficient, motivating and inspiring them? When the interviewer smiles and asks back, "Well, what do you think?" you have an invitation to show the depth of your management thinking.

*You start with a solid foundation. I hire my team for their skills, provide them with the best possible equipment, teach them to constantly improve processes, and fight for their interests. I can give you examples of each of these.*

*If a team senses loyalty from a manager, they'll give it back. If a manager is open to suggestion, eager to grow the team's talents and responsibilities as well as his own, and sets consistent goals, they'll be motivated to emulate him. I am very clear that performance matters, so I don't make excuses or dodge responsibility. When we have missed a goal—and it happens to everyone—I help the team confront reality and improve. People on my team don't accept passive negativity—nobody says, "Well, we couldn't do anything about it."*

**Related questions:**
- ▶ *Tell me about a time you made your team more effective, either through improving efficiency or through some other means.*

- ▶ **If you get this job, you will supervise the lowest-performing team in the company. What would you do in the first month to improve it?**
- ▶ **When has your team failed due to circumstances beyond its control?**

## Tell me how you measure the results of your work.

"If you can measure it, you can manage it," goes the business truism, and you want to be as concrete as possible. If you use S.M.A.R.T. goals or other structured, objective ways to measure success, start your answer with that. Managers' claims to success must stand up to scrutiny. Did you establish objective success standards? Did you communicate measurable goals to your staff? Did everyone have a stake in your team's success?

Don't substitute anecdotal or qualitative opinion for objective measurement. If you have not measured results in the past, analyze past work before the interview, and ask questions about the employer's standards.

*The bottom line of advertising is, which idea sells the product better, and so I keep my Web creative team "honest" by carefully monitoring the response rates of ads with different approaches. Any ad that doesn't get a 0.75 percent click-through rate gets pulled, no matter how much we love it. I also base our bonus program in part on maintaining that overall rate.*

**Related questions:**
- ▶ **Other than promotions or money, what objective evidence can you offer that you have been successful?**
- ▶ **How do you establish benchmarks?**
- ▶ **What do you believe are the critical success factors for this position?**

## How would you decide between two courses of action?

*Decide* is the key word here, because managers are defined by their decisions, not by waffling, and "gut feel" decision making is hard for an interviewer to trust. Can you describe a structured decision-making process? Can you tell when you need more information? Can you make priorities early in the process, listen to different opinions, and then apply decisions that are wise and fair? Can you then rally a staff around an unpopular decision?

*First, I define the objective clearly. With my staff, I set priorities based on short- and long-term business plans. For example, if we have to choose between short-term revenue and long-term risk management, how do we choose? Then I require my staff to come up with objective criteria. We project best- and worst-case scenarios. When all that's in place, we gather the right data—and the correct course of action almost always emerges from plugging that data into the scenarios we've constructed. Let me give you an example. . . .*

**Related questions:**
  ▶ *If your team was divided on what course of action to take, what would you do?*
  ▶ *Describe a time you made a gut call. What were the circumstances and what was the result?*

## Tell me about a time you suddenly had to do more with less.

Perhaps an important person on your team dropped out suddenly. Maybe your budget was slashed, or your quota was raised unexpectedly. Your story should tell as much about your attitude as your ability.

*I remember an unexpected problem sixteen months ago. One week after my company announced a hiring freeze my boss announced he was leaving. A team member left with him. A temporary manager was assigned part-time, but her plate was so full I decided to take the following initiatives to make sure my department hit its goals without burning out. . . .*

**Related questions:**
  ▶ *Have you ever contributed directly to increased productivity?*
  ▶ *When did you have to take on new responsibility without giving up any part of your old job?*

# How have current business trends affected this company's results?

This tests your research and your work habits. Do you keep up with industry news, and can you relate it to this business? Less experienced candidates can use this question to show their capacity for growth. Your research should include big issues like trade, regulation, competition, and technology.

*Fortune magazine said last week that increasing energy prices are squeezing profits in this industry. You can't raise prices fast enough to keep up with the cost of energy in this part of the country. Here's how I worked on this problem during the energy price spike of 2003–2004. . . .*

**Related questions:**
- ▶ *What do you think our industry's most important problem is today?*
- ▶ *If hired, how would you help us to stay abreast of current trends?*

# How have you learned about your customers?

First, describe how you found reliable information. Objective, structured methods like surveys, focus groups, and the like are stronger than simple observations. This makes for dry narrative, though, so also talk about personal contact. Describe both types of customers— the people or businesses who pay for your services, and the people who rely on you at work.

*Every retail product company has two layers of customers: the retail outlets are where we do business with the consumers who pay for our footwear. I used focus groups to make the retail displays of our product more user-friendly, which I'll tell you more about in a minute. I also spend a lot of time shopping anonymously in sporting goods stores. I ask customers to recommend a running shoe, and listen carefully to the reasons they like a certain brand. Then I have more formal meetings with the store managers. During those conversations, I check the focus group findings against the managers' experience.*

**Related questions:**
- ▶ *Have you gathered objective data about your customers?*
- ▶ *Tell me about a time a customer surprised you. What did you learn?*
- ▶ *How fast can you implement a customer-suggested improvement?*

## According to your direct reports, what kind of manager are you?

Management is not a popularity contest. Similar to the question in chapter 3 asking how a best friend or spouse would describe you, this question can divert you into thinking about relationships. Focus on how you get things done through a staff, especially in the context of specific challenges. You can make many legitimate claims here; just be certain to have a concrete example backing up each one.

*My direct reports would tell you that my strength in delegation makes them feel not just included but effective. I prefer achievement-oriented people, so I knock down external barriers to their achievement. I walk them through my own decision-making process as a way of coaching them; often I'll pose a dilemma to them and ask for a recommendation. My staff would tell you that I expect them to make commitments carefully but fulfill them unconditionally. To that end, I provide the skills and information they need to become A-level players. For example, when I had to develop new performance goals for my team, I took them offsite, told them the required result, and spent the day hammering out concrete goals with each person.*

**Related questions:**
- ▶ *What do peers expect from you as a manager?*
- ▶ *How would your staff say you've changed/grown over the last two years?*

## My Best Advice

I typically start every management interview saying that I want the candidate to take fifteen minutes and tell me everything about themselves and their life that they think is important to me in considering them for employment. What will demonstrate their probability of success? I expect them to fill up the fifteen minutes, and if they stop after five, I tell them they have ten more minutes, so keep going. If they start to go beyond fifteen minutes I tell them to stop.

This tells me what they know about themselves, and what they think is important. If they've done homework on me, on our business and the job, they will put their work history in the context of what's going to be important to us. It also tells me if they can speak extemporaneously for fifteen minutes. Can they be concise and focus on the important factors? That's very important for managers.

—*Mike Durik, executive vice president, Kelly Services*

## Additional Management Questions

### How do you develop your employees?

Choose situations in which you have set specific and measurable objectives for staff, then given them the resources to grow. How frequently do you give feedback, and in what form? Do you "give away your job" to your team, so that you are also able to grow, or do you have to motivate people who are not going to be promoted soon? Do you believe that A-level people are made or born . . . or something else? Are you a critic, a cheerleader, or a coach?

**Related questions:**
▶ *Describe the weakest performer on your team. How have you helped this person improve?*
▶ *Tell me how you would train your replacement.*
▶ *This is an underperforming department. What would you do about that?*

# What qualities do you look for in an ideal employee?

Describe both skills and motivations of people you'd want on your staff. Give cultural clues, such as work values. Can you hire someone who is better than you at some task? Use this opening to talk about the team itself—how you keep it balanced, growing, and responsible, and what the company's expectations are. If you're coming into a turnaround situation, carefully judge expectations as to timing, firing, budget, and results.

**Related questions:**
- ▶ *What are your priorities for hiring?*
- ▶ *If you had to pick one skill you'd always demand in an employee, what would it be?*
- ▶ *Rank the top five technical skills for someone reporting to you.*

# How much supervision do you require?

Describe how you "manage upward" to your superiors by keeping them proactively informed, by spotting potential problems early, and by delivering solutions, not just problems. Do you actively seek feedback? Employers value the manager who can deliver just the right amount of information without constant check-in. Discuss how much feedback you need to do your job, and your desire to get feedback in order to grow.

**Related questions:**
- ▶ *At what point do you tell you supervisor bad news?*
- ▶ *Have you ever wished you had more feedback from your manager?*

# How do you promote excellence in your organization?

*Excellence* is an easy word to abuse, so first define excellence in the context of the business goals. Be candid about the challenge of exceptional performance. Cite obstacles you've experienced, and how you overcame them. Tell about rewarding great performance, and using failure as a turning point to galvanize improved performance.

Finally, prove that you apply standards of excellence to your own performance—with specific goals.

**Related questions:**
- ▶ *Tell me how you reward someone who exceeds your expectations.*
- ▶ *Our company is not what you'd call an industry leader. How would you improve its performance?*
- ▶ *Tell me about a situation in which you had to deliver negative feedback to an employee. How did you approach the conversation?*

## Tell me about a time when circumstances dictated a change of plan.

Pull out one of your best achievement stories, and detail how you designed a flexible project plan at the outset. Scale is important with this question, so choose a major change, not just a minor adjustment to your plans. Were you able to change processes without wasting completed work? Did you communicate clearly and quickly with key people above, below, and in other departments?

It's dangerous to blame superiors for change here. Change happens all the time. Managers who can face it head-on, without whining or blaming, are highly valued.

**Related questions:**
- ▶ *Have you ever come close to a goal, only to have the goal change?*
- ▶ *How do you manage the ever-changing environment of technology?*
- ▶ *Tell me about a role that required you to be flexible, whether it was with work plans, deadlines, priorities, or people.*

## How would you implement performance measurements?

If you have experience with these, briefly describe them *and* why you believe they are effective—or not—at your current or former employer.

Then talk about the implementation itself. Does your staff have objective and achievable goals, and do you focus on improvement for all? Describe how you arrived at those goals, and why they're the right ones. Can you deliver uncomfortable feedback constructively? Finally, do your performance reviews actually result in *better performance?*

**Related questions:**
- ▶ *What is the purpose of a performance review?*
- ▶ *Tell me about a time you taught discipline to a wavering, unfocused staff member.*
- ▶ *How often do you praise your people for a job well done?*
- ▶ *What's the most effective habit for improving performance day to day?*

## What tasks do you delegate and what tasks do you reserve for yourself?

*How* and *why* you delegate tasks are the hidden questions here. A strong manager distributes work according to staff skills, responsibility, and growth potential, in order to free herself to do work that others cannot do. Your success as a manager depends on your ability to get much more done than you can by yourself, which also means supervising, coaching, and increasing the skills of staff to whom work is delegated.

**Related questions:**
- ▶ *How do you manage multiple projects?*
- ▶ *Tell me about a time you grew one of your staff by giving them more responsibility. How did you do it? What was the result?*
- ▶ *Describe to me your system for assigning tasks to employees. Who gets the fun tasks, and who gets the drudge work?*

## Tell me about an unpopular decision you had to make.

What pressures did you face? Were your superiors or peers displeased? Perspective is important here, so describe the consequences of the unpopular decision and don't exaggerate. What, finally, was the result of your decision? Was it worth the cost? Your interviewer will carefully judge the candor and openness of your story.

Describe the people affected by the decision: Do they view your decision as principled, consistent, honest, and fair? Do they know you listened to alternative solutions, and feel heard? Do they feel they are shouldering the consequences? Arbitrary decisions damage morale and decisions seen as pursuing a hidden agenda crush loyalty.

**Related questions:**
- ▶ *We like consensus here. Ever have a time when you couldn't reach agreement with a superior?*
- ▶ *How have you led your staff to complete a project they did not want to do?*

## How do you make meetings productive?

"Death by meeting" is familiar managerial agony. Do you have the discipline to make meetings productive? Discuss the importance of preparation, directed leadership (e.g., sticking to the agenda), delegation of subissues, and ending with tasks, timelines, and responsibilities clearly defined. If you have rapport with the interviewer, turn the tables and discuss the remaining agenda for this interview.

**Related questions:**
- ▶ *What do you do when a discussion gets off-track?*
- ▶ *How do you prepare for a presentation in front of your superiors?*

## How do you contribute to your company's budgeting process?

There are significant technical skills and knowledge implied in this question. If you really understand the budgeting process, and if you're really skilled in financial tracking, analysis, etc., then detail your role. This can lead to a much larger conversation, so check in with questions like, "Am I explaining this in enough detail?" and "Is there a similar process in place here?"

Your claims of budgeting skill can be quickly verified here, so be candid. If you don't contribute much to the budgeting process, say why not. Perhaps it's something you look forward to doing in the next job. This is a chance to ask what the learning opportunity might be.

**Related questions:**
- ▶ *How can you make sure a department or project budget is realistic and on track?*
- ▶ *How do you handle major expenses or cost deviations?*
- ▶ *Have you ever created a budget from scratch? Tell me the process.*

## What Were They Thinking?

I was conducting a mock interview with one of the most impressive soon-to-graduate MBAs. He was loaded with brains, determination, and charm, and had the accomplishments to prove it . . . but he bombed when I asked the seemingly innocuous question of "Why this college?"

He took off on a tirade about how he *could* have gone to Harvard but his school was every bit as good as Harvard and what was so special about Harvard anyway? His sour-grapes attitude made me imagine someone who would blow his stack in high-stress management situations.

Clearly, I had hit a nerve—and one that could be his undoing. Over-reaction is a killer in management interviews, where they're testing your ability to stay focused and in control.

—*University career coach Kate Kavanagh*

I see from your resume that you haven't lasted longer than two years in any position. Are you a job-hopper or were you fired each time?"

Melanie, a 28-year old attorney, had anticipated this question from the moment she and Frank had met. The senior partner's tactic was clear: throw candidates off-stride with aggressive, even hostile questions. He didn't make small talk, he didn't smile. He sat behind his desk and glowered.

She smiled confidently, and leaned slightly toward Frank. "I define a job-hopper as someone without a passion for their work—someone too focused on grabbing the next position for an extra hundred bucks a week," she said. "My resume shows a steady accumulation of skills and expertise in a fast-moving market, and while I have outgrown jobs in the past, I believe this position and this company offer ample room for growth."

She continued. "I also understand that the pace of change in business is accelerating. That's why I have focused on learning and taking on new responsibilities at the same time I have delivered exceptional work. A lawyer who doesn't look for new challenges every couple of years can be a drag on a fast-moving firm like this one."

Frank gave her a prosecutor's stare, and replied, "But you'd just as soon leave us if you don't get a promotion every two years?"

"Not at all," said Melanie. "I simply assume that no one can guarantee a job position these days. That's why I never stand still. I'm looking for a place to grow into a position of leadership." She concluded, "I think that's called ambition."

Good under pressure, Frank thought, and made a note on Melanie's resume: "Not a job-hopper, but motivated to move up. J.O.T.": Just our type.

Ah, the stress interview—the job candidate's nightmare! It comes in many forms from mildly provocative to sadistic. Its purpose: to put candidates on the defensive. Its logic: (1) Stressful situations show the "true person" under a polished preparation; and (2) Candidates who perform well under pressure in the interview will perform well under pressure in the job.

Stress interviews aren't perpetrated by creeps who want to see you squirm (even if they feel like that). They're a legitimate and effective reflection of work, which is so often . . . *stressful*. The candidate who handles interview pressure with confidence and grace goes light-years past the candidate who can handle only the easy questions.

Stress interviews come in several forms:

**Painful or aggressive questions:** Even a mild-mannered interviewer can put you on the spot by asking a question like "Why were you fired?" These questions are intended to trigger your self-doubts, but if you see the underlying game you can use them to project an aura of confidence.

**Aggressive attitude or behavior:** Some interviewers have a cultish faith in a tough attitude. They adopt a "show me" attitude in their words, facial expression, body language, and behavior. You're supposed to believe their behavior is your fault, as if you were a naughty child. This is a potent act and many qualified candidates blow the interview because they become flustered by aggressive behavior.

**Unexpected behaviors:** This tactic is similar to courtroom theatrics. The interviewer tries to throw you off with unexpected behaviors. For example, an interviewer might ask the same technical question several times, pretending not to understand your answer. You explain several times, each time getting more exasperated at their "stupidity."

Guess what they're testing—not your ability to answer a technical question but your ability to communicate to someone who isn't technical! (A variation of this technique: an interviewer deliberately insists that an incorrect answer is the right one.)

**Brainteasers or puzzle interviews:** "Puzzle" questions are becoming more popular. You are not expected to know the actual answer to questions like "How much does all the ice in a hockey rink weigh?" but you are expected to explain how you would find out. Obscure facts are less important than your ability to think quickly, analyze the problem, arrive at a conclusion, and explain your logic. Sometimes the stress they inflict is of the "Jeez, I should know that!" variety ("Why are traffic lights green at the bottom and red at the top?") and sometimes the questions are even bogus ("Why are traffic lights red at the bottom and green at the top?"). Often the questions literally have no correct answer, for example, "If you had to get rid of one state, which would it be?" Famously used at Microsoft, puzzle questions are believed to be especially good at helping select candidates in technology and other rapidly changing fields.

**Case interviews:** The case interview tests candidates at a high level, usually for business or technical positions. Briefly, you are presented with an open-ended business situation—usually a dilemma or set of hard choices—and required to describe a path toward a solution. Interviewers note your knowledge of relevant business issues, quantitative and analytical skills, ability to prioritize and anticipate problems, and communication skills.

The case interview also tests your ability to overcome stage fright! As a candidate stands at the whiteboard working on the problem, additional stress factors include limited information, limited time, and constant questioning of assumptions ("Why do you assume that there would be little impact on costs at that point?"). At the end of the case, the candidate is expected to make a recommendation. A variation for advanced candidates: "Devise a case study for this company. What's a critical situation now, and how would we go about solving it?"

Although the formats differ, stress interviews demand one common response: keep cool. This is where your confidence—and your ability to detach emotionally from the interviewer—will truly be tested. If you become flustered, your mind will fog over with apprehension, which is exactly what you *don't* want.

The key methods to use when asked stress questions are similar to those used in high-level negotiation:

- Clarify the question and the nature of the answer desired (this can also buy you some time to think). What are they trying to get at?
- Communicate what you're thinking and doing.
- State assumptions and ask for unknown information.
- Focus on the way in which you're solving the problem, not necessarily the "right" answer.
- If you answer with a story, don't get so lost in the story that you lose the point. (For this reason, it's best to go with a story you prepared in advance—see chapter 6 and also "Mastering the Freestyle Interview," page 3.)
- Be open, honest, and direct, but refuse to be emotionally intimidated. (Like playground dogs, aggressive interviewers can smell fear.)

Only you know which questions will feel most stressful to you. Some questions in this chapter will seem relatively easy . . . and others excruciating. Part of the stress interview game is controlling your own anxiety; you can take the attitude that "anything you say can and will be used against you," or you can view the stress interview as an exciting challenge.

Be aware that stress interviewers can be deceptive. The person who asks brutally tough questions might turn out to be warmhearted and easygoing . . . after you are hired!

## What If Disaster Strikes?

There's another kind of stressful interview, and that's the one that feels like a disaster. The interview is such a slippery, human conversation that sometimes bad interviews can happen to even the best candidates. You can sense when the interview is slipping rapidly downhill: the interviewer is losing interest, or openly hostile, or trying to shut down the interview after ten minutes. If you think an interview is going terribly, it probably is.

But here's the good news: in this nightmare scenario, you have nothing to lose by changing the game. When you sense disaster, the best tactic is to confront it candidly. Say, for example, "Excuse me, but I don't think this interview is going very well. Do you agree?" If the interviewer says, "You're right, it's not," you are done. They will probably tell you that you will not get the job. Remain positive and allow them to close the interview. Often, however, the interviewer will say, "No, maybe we just got off-track," and you can reply, "You're right. I feel like we missed a beat on that second question. May I try that again?"

If you deal directly with an interview that's going downhill, you have a 50-50 shot at getting back on track. Some interviewers will keep a poker face, and you won't have any idea what they think. Often, however, your openness will snap the interviewer out of his or her negative feeling. For example, she or he may say, "You know, you're not right for this job but I like your experience, and maybe there's a job for you in another department." Even if it doesn't result in a job, the fact that you changed the interview from negative to positive says good things about you.

The worst tactic for dealing with disaster is to continue through a declining interview as if everything were fine. Practically speaking, you're wasting both your time and the interviewer's. Nobody wins, and most important, their negative assessment of you won't change.

So, if you feel that sense of dread that things are going very wrong, call attention to it and ask how you can get back into a positive conversation. It's the only path back from disaster.

## Stress Interview Questions and Answers

### Tell me about a time when you were in over your head.

If you've never been in over your head, you are underemployed. In fact, the most confident employees relish "impossible" challenges, and sometimes fail. The story you tell must relate a significant challenge and show your persistence, motivation, and calm attitude toward responsibility, as well as an understanding of what can and cannot be changed in a situation—in brief, a mature perspective. Shifting blame for failure, or conceding defeat too quickly, is not acceptable.

*I accepted a new position as project manager for services delivered to a big client, and two weeks later my boss left the company. The project was in serious trouble—late and over budget—and the client wasn't in the mood to hear excuses. I could see that I wouldn't be able to come up to speed fast enough, so swallowing my pride, I briefed the senior vice president on the situation. We immediately flew out to Kansas City to work out a solution with the client; I continued to act as the contact and project manager, and also identified peers who could contribute to a solution. The most important lesson I learned was to set my eagerness to please aside, face brutal reality, and relentlessly drive toward a solution.*

### Related questions:
- ▶ *Have you ever failed at a job because of someone else's poor performance?*
- ▶ *If you could rework one project that failed, what would it be and how would you do things differently?*

## Tell me about a time you really messed up.

Think of a time you grew from criticism, and display your professional attitude. Do not use a story that excuses your behavior, but instead show you are accountable for your mistakes.

*My manager had assigned me to interview a star athlete for a company publication. I tried for several weeks, calling his agent, calling his lawyer, but I never got that interview. As the deadline approached, I just quoted a bland statement the athlete had made a year before. My manager was frankly disappointed and clearly let me know it. I took responsibility for the mistake, and instead of just promising it wouldn't happen again, asked if he would help me to develop alternative strategies when I was stuck like that again. It turned into a good conversation about growing my interviewing skills.*

**Related questions:**

▶ *Tell me about a time when someone verbally gave you negative feedback. How did you receive this feedback? How did you respond to the speaker?*

▶ *Tell me about a time you disappointed your manager.*

▶ *Ever just blown an assignment big time?*

## Aren't you overqualified for this job?

Overqualified to do what—perform the job's duties, grow quickly into greater responsibility, and deliver superior results? The hidden question: are you just settling for this job, and will you leave the moment something better comes along? This question is often asked of more senior candidates, in which case it often translates as, "You make too much money!"

Briefly review your qualifications and then focus the rest of your answer on the advantages of hiring someone with your range of experience. You might also probe for underlying questions (such as their anticipation that you will cost too much). Point out that you're interested in a long-term, mutually beneficial relationship. Feeling really confident? Ask if the interviewer has hired a qualified person who then stalled and never grew . . . and then point out you're prepared to be a top player today.

*If by "overqualified" you mean that my skills and experience for this job are greater than other applicants', I think that's in my favor. By hiring me, you get someone with much less ramp-up time, someone able to take on more responsibility than others. I want to find a job in a company that wants to find and hire the best employees it possibly can.*

*In addition, I've seen mistakes made in this business that less experienced candidates haven't, thus I can prevent them from happening. Do you have any specific concerns about my level of expertise?*

**Related questions:**

▶ *Why shouldn't I hire someone less expensive?*

▶ *Why are you applying for a job I think of as . . . beneath you?*

## Aren't you underqualified?

This is a classic attempt to throw you off your stride, but it's also a great chance to project confidence. (If you're not qualified, why are they talking to you?) Go straight to your key messages, tailored carefully to the job. If you are changing careers, ask them to confirm your assertions: "I've proved I can do this part of the job—don't you agree?" Don't exaggerate similarities between this job and the last.

*Not at all. A hotel reservations agent screens guest requests and sells additional services. I've taken orders and "up-sold" customers in a retail environment. You require meticulous attention to detail because your reputation depends on getting reservations right. I'd like to tell you a story that proves my attention to detail. . . . Given those skills, tell me how quickly must a reservations agent be up to speed—I learn fast, as my references will tell you.*

*Also, I'm looking forward to learning constantly about the business. What career growth do you see for a top performer over, say, three years?*

**Related questions:**
- ► **Doesn't your lack of experience in this field mean you can't do the job?**
- ► **How in the world do you expect to move from a career in sales to a job in health care administration?**

## Tell me why you left your last job.

If you were fired or laid off, this is one time you don't want to volunteer details. You also must avoid criticizing your last employer, so keep a positive tone as you relate the facts. Accept your responsibility and conclude with a forward-looking statement that focuses on the current opportunity.[4]

*The special education program where I worked decided to create a community outreach program. I applied for the director's job, stating that I was more interested in designing and running a program than in clinical work. They hired someone else, and told me that, since my clear plan was not to do clinical work forever, I had better start looking elsewhere. The experience*

[4] For a structured way to craft such a statement, see *Monster Careers: How to Land the Job of Your Life*, pages 135–139.

left me convinced that school management is my future, and in addition to my clinical experience, I have much to learn. That's why I'm applying for this assistant director's position.

**Related questions:**
- ▶ *Walk me through all the times you've left a job. Were the reasons similar or different? (Hint: Describe your career as a thoughtful search for the right place to grow.)*
- ▶ *Have you ever been fired? When and why? (Hint: If you were fired more than two jobs ago, this is much less relevant. Give a short answer.)*
- ▶ *What would cause you to leave the job we're discussing?*

## What is your greatest weakness?

This is a moment to be open, honest, and direct. Although candidates typically try to spin a weakness into a strength by saying, "I'm a perfectionist" or "I overwork," employers have heard these ploys a thousand times. Everyone has growth areas; the compelling candidate shows self-awareness and a desire to improve. Don't stray into irrelevant personal weaknesses (like your little online-shopping addiction). Instead, identify your weakest point in the job's *noncritical* qualities, and outline your plan for overcoming it.

*My last public relations job was in a company so big that we never had to drum up coverage; my priority was to respond to hundreds of media inquiries. Because this company is much smaller and a little "off the radar," a public relations manager here will have to reach out to the media to get any coverage. I plan to introduce myself quickly to the opinion makers in this industry, and I believe the public relations skills we've discussed will help me deliver on those relationships quickly when they're established.*

**Related questions:**
- ▶ *What would your references say is your greatest weakness? (Hint: Refer a work reference—someone who has seen you perform—not a personal reference.)*
- ▶ *Have you identified any areas for self-improvement?*
- ▶ *All of us have pluses and minuses in our performance. What minuses can we expect from you?*

## What criticism do you have in regard to your present employer?

This is actually a character question. Are you a complainer? A gossip? Can you keep confidences? Saying "My boss loses his temper over trivia" spins you toward the door (even if it's true).

You can't say "None," however, so keep your criticism business-like. It's a great opportunity to show you're a big-picture person. Balance criticism and praise. You might cite examples (if asked) in areas such as organization, business methods, strategy, or process.

*ABC Co. became the market leader by offering superior products, but it doesn't have a great reputation for service to existing customers. I believe they are leaving money on the table by not making it easier for existing customers to upgrade or enhance the products they've bought. Just a simple change, such as reducing waiting time at the phone center, would help a lot. I'm hopeful that they're going to do that soon; it will definitely help top-line revenue. Would you tell me about your company's process for handling customer inquiries?*

**Related questions:**
  ▶ *How would you handle it if someone were to openly criticize or make unfavorable comments about your company and its products?*
  ▶ *If you were to make one change in your current company, what would it be?*

## Tell me about a time when you were pressured to reveal sensitive or confidential information.

They want to know if you're trustworthy, and how you handle personal pressure. Did you maintain a productive relationship with the person pressing for information, or did you become self-righteous and embarrass them with a lecture? What if they were in a position of authority? What if they were a close friend? If possible, tell a story in which you refused to divulge information but preserved a working relationship. (Incidentally, you must redirect or decline to answer any interview question in cases when the law requires nondisclosure of inside information.)

*I believe trustworthiness is earned hard and lost easily. I went to a meeting in my boss's place, during which someone indiscreetly mentioned an impending layoff. A good friend was in the affected group, and later she asked me directly if I knew anything about the rumors. I told her I heard rumors but knew nothing specific. When she asked again I altered the conversation by asking what she had heard and suggesting we all had to be prepared for changes. That led to a much more productive conversation about how to work well during all the uncertainty.*

**Related questions:**
- ▶ **Tell me about a time you had to keep a big company secret.**
- ▶ **This is a sensitive position. How do you react when you learn something you shouldn't know?**
- ▶ **If your supervisor told you to lie to a customer, would you do that?**

## Tell me about the last time you had an unsatisfied customer. How did you handle this?

You must answer this question with a story; what-ifs won't do. Demonstrate that you can show respect and courtesy even to a customer who needs to vent their anger. You must show that you can offer solutions without automatically punting the irate customer up to your manager.

*The most important factor is to take responsibility without losing my cool, and to reassure the customer that my job is to move the problem to a satisfactory solution. Last year, I had a customer who brought back a toy bought on sale that simply didn't work. We don't take returns on sale items. I could see he was angrier about his child's disappointment than the money, so I suggested the following. . . .*

**Related questions:**
- ▶ **Is the customer always right? What if she's wrong?**
- ▶ **How far will you go to satisfy an upset customer?**

### Have you ever found yourself in a critical situation that required immediate action?

What was the situation? What did you do? What was the outcome? Describe the process by which you arrived at a quick—and correct—decision. Did you think two steps ahead? Did you keep the right people informed? Did you persuade others to take the right actions?

*We were catering a company picnic at the beach for a big client. It was a Sunday night, and I was working with just two others. Well, because of a crack in the refrigeration system, all the hamburgers, chicken, dairy—the whole thing—had warmed up to a cool room temperature. I had one hour to serve the food. I decided that even though the risk was low, I wasn't going to chance a spoilage problem. I called my boss and left a message that I was going to get forty pizzas from two local places. Then I talked to the customer, who was disappointed but appreciated our "no compromise" food safety policy. Then I made a big, pretty funny announcement down on the beach that we were turning it into a pizza party. Their kids actually loved it.*

**Related questions:**
- ▶ *Tell me about a crisis.*
- ▶ *Can you think of a situation in which you lost money for the company by doing the right thing?*

### Sell me this pencil.

You can put a new shine on this dusty old sales question (and others like it) by asserting your key messages throughout the conversation. The interviewer can tell from your record that you can sell products. Today, he wants to know if you can sell yourself. Are you persuasive? Can you quickly tailor your answer to the situation? Do you merely repeat your resume points or do you begin to build a relationship? Here are three approaches:

*I increased sales at my last company by 35 percent in a year, and let me tell you, one of the most important tools for increasing my productivity was a pencil just like this one. . . .*

OR

*I can see you're considering using this pencil. I was confronted by this kind of decision last year, and let me tell you how a simple thing like a pencil can improve productivity, increase sales, and save money. . . .*

OR

*Do you mind if I ask you a question about your job? When I was called on to increase sales, I had to determine what, of all things, I needed to help me do that. You'd be surprised, but I found that a lot of little things, like the quality of my tools, made that difference. Take this pencil, for example, which is so reliable I could forget about whether it worked or not and focus on more important things. My question to you is, do you need that kind of reliability?*

**Related questions:**
- ▶ **Persuade me to spend $10,000 upgrading my office.**
- ▶ **I believe minivans are for losers. Change my mind.**

## My Best Advice

Even senior candidates can have disastrous answers to open-ended questions like "design a house for me." If the person jumps in and starts designing a home in their mind and then writes it on the board without asking questions ("Is this in the mountains? The seashore? Is it for a family or single occupancy? Do we need to take handicapped access into consideration?"), they miss the point. The interviewer doesn't want a house, but wants to know how you would approach a design issue. If you ask questions to frame the problem, you'll always do better.

I've had some people tell me they want the job so bad they'll just answer in a way they think the interviewer wants to hear rather than being themselves. If you do that, you're going to have a tough struggle.

—Lisa Cornay-Albright, Microsoft Corporation

# Additional Questions

**How many quarters—placed one on top of the other—would it take to reach the top of the Empire State Building?**

Simple arithmetic? Not quite. This puzzle question contains a hidden data point that you must ascertain first—what is meant by the phrase "placed one on top of the other"? Does that mean stacked like poker chips or placed end-to-end? After asking the question, the answer is in fact simple arithmetic (estimate the diameter or thickness of a quarter, calculate how many make a foot in length, and multiply by the height, in feet, of the building). The point is not arriving at a correct figure, but asking the right questions and showing a logical approach. (For bonus points, you might also ask if the basement, technically part of the building, should be included, and whether you're measuring to the top floor, or to the top of the spire.)

**Related questions:**
- ▶ *How many peas would it take to fill the New Orleans Superdome?*
- ▶ *How would you weigh a moving train?*

**You are in charge of marketing a huge new 12-cylinder SUV. It gets twelve miles per gallon, while the competition's SUV gets twenty-one. In the months leading up to the car's introduction, an international crisis causes gasoline prices to triple. What do you do?**

Case questions like this are grounded in real-life issues that require action, so an academic "either–or" recommendation is not satisfactory. Identify and confirm the most important factors of the problem ("We don't know when gas prices will fall again. It would take two years to raise the mileage of the vehicle; thus the central conflict will not go away soon. Are those assumptions correct?") Then analyze the situation based on those factors. Explain your use of facts, logic, and quantitative analysis to solve the problem. You might wish to explore creative solutions, but also describe how you would measure their risk factors. Do not rest your case on open-ended recommendations— you must state what the company should do to achieve its goals and be willing to live with the result.

**Related questions:**
  ▶ *The board of this residential treatment center has voted to expand our capacity by 50 percent. Unfortunately, the only land abutting our property might be designated as an official wetland next year. Take me to our goal.*
  ▶ *We see a huge opportunity to buy into a new business but have to move fast. Our stock price, however, has fallen so far that we cannot make an acquisition based on stock valuation. What do we do?*
  ▶ *Your job will be to improve efficiency in this department. Tell me in detail how you will do that.*

## You've been brought in to rescue a project that is certain to miss its deadline. What do you do?

You can't buy your way out of every problem, so offering monetary incentives to the team won't work. You can't accept failure. This question tests not only your crisis management skills, but your ability to preserve the long-term morale of the people involved. How does this project relate to the big picture? Who has promised what to whom? Describe how you would assess the key problems, gain the commitment of the team members, alert management without passing the buck, and quickly present a recommendation with buy-in from all parties involved (including the customer, if they're involved). Summon resources to document your work and prevent such a slippage from happening again.

**Related questions:**
  ▶ *Tell me about a time you were given an impossible, thankless task.*
  ▶ *You are about to disappoint our biggest customer . . . for the second time this year. Pick up the phone and tell them about it.*

## Tell me about this 2-year gap in your employment history.

Candidates sweat a lot over this question: "If they know I was unemployed that long, they'll think I'm a loser!" In fact, how you handle the question makes as much of an impression as the details. Be truthful but upbeat about long unemployment—tell what you learned, how you persevered, what extra lengths you went to fulfill financial responsibilities like repaying student loans. Someone who took a temporary job to pay the bills can make a stronger impression than someone who hopped through five inappropriate jobs because they were desperate.

Some circumstances require more detailed explanation: If you deliberately stepped out of the workforce, you must explain why (whether you were in school, in prison, on vacation, at home with young children, or writing your novel). Note how the experience prepared you for the job at hand. You don't have to bare your soul in response to this question; just fill the information gap.

**Related questions:**
- ▶ *So, let me get this right—you were on vacation for eighteen months?*
- ▶ *You went back to school to get an MBA, but this job doesn't require one. Why did you spend all that time and money if you weren't going to get the benefit?*

## Tell me about a conflict you've had with management. How did you handle it and how was it resolved?

Breathe. Chuckle.

They're judging your emotional control and sense of professional detachment as you relate the story. Can you describe the conflict from the other side's point of view? Did you allow disagreement to affect your work? How proactive were you in seeking a solution? Did you protect those to whom you were responsible? Describe how you patiently sought a resolution based on facts, company culture, and other nonemotional factors. Stay cool as you describe the incident and its resolution.

Do not cite conflict as the principal reason why you are looking for a new position unless the other side's behavior was egregiously wrong. In that case, you can ask if that behavior would be tolerated in your new workplace.

Related questions:
- ▶ *What makes you angry?*
- ▶ *If there's one thing that management does to annoy you, what is it?*

## Who would you describe as a "problem" person? How do you deal with them?

If you name real people, stick a label on them, and reveal prejudice, you are an HR director's nightmare and you will not get the job. If you discuss "problem" behaviors with an open mind, and prove that you can work with many persons and many styles, you are on the right track. Put angry or hurt feelings to one side. Demonstrate that you can focus on common work challenges from people of different backgrounds or interests. If you have a story about overcoming a conflict in cooperation with someone else, tell it.

Then inquire why the question was asked. The interviewer might have someone in mind (like your next boss).

Related questions:
- ▶ *How would you deal with a high-strung personality?*
- ▶ *Tell me about a staff member of yours who just won't cooperate or take direction.*

## I don't think people who go to state schools do particularly well in this field. What do you think?

Depending on whether you went to a state school, the interviewer might be trying to intimidate you, or trick you into revealing a prejudice. They might be revealing their own bias. Don't take the bait: point out that you don't like to generalize, but focus on skills, experience, character, and performance in your judgment of people.

**Related questions:**

▶ *I'm not sure [an older person/woman/gay person/ Catholic/younger person/recovering addict et al.] would feel comfortable leading this team. Do you agree?*

▶ *You came from XYZ Co.; I hope you're not what they would describe as an "XYZ type of person."*

## What Were They Thinking?

As an executive recruiter, I did a confidential search for a packaged-goods company that had quietly decided to replace its president. Only the board of directors knew. One candidate I met seemed very strong, but a little bit desperate to leave his current job. I wasn't sure he could handle the stress of the new job. Of course, we don't reveal the names of the companies we work with, so all he knew was that it was a packaged-goods company in the greater metropolitan area.

So in this stressful situation, he panics. Without telling us, he calls up every packaged-goods company in the area, gets the head of HR, and says, "Hi, I believe that your organization is looking for a new president and I'm being considered as a candidate. I don't have many slots available on my calendar, but I'd like to arrange an interview." Pretty soon, thirty-eight firms hear a rumor that their president is leaving—and every one of them is calling me! And I'm thinking, who *is* this guy?

When an organization sees that kind of behavior, they kill the candidate right away. They see the candidate as being uncontrollable . . . and he is! Would you trust your future to a person like that?

—*Brian Gard of executive search firm Avenue Rhodes*

# 9 Six Unique Interview Formats

**SCENE: Angela's apartment in Colorado Springs. Ten-twenty A.M. The phone rings.**

ANGELA: Hello?

EMPLOYER: May I speak to Angela Wayne?

ANGELA: This is Angela.

EMPLOYER: Angela, this is Nick Pappas of SellCorp. I'm calling because I found your resume in our database, and I have an amazing opportunity in my finance department. I wonder if you are in the market for a new position now?

ANGELA: I'm glad you called! Yes, I'm looking for a new finance position. I know about SellCorp but I didn't know you were adding people. Can you tell me about the position?

NICK: We haven't posted this job yet; it's a senior position in Accounts Payable. Before I tell you about the job, may I ask a few questions?

ANGELA: Certainly. Let me grab a pen.

[Angela walks to her desk in the corner of her apartment. Standing, she writes "SellCorp—Nick Pappas" on a yellow pad of paper.]

NICK: Your resume states that you've had three years of experience. Is that correct?

ANGELA: That's correct—three years last month. Since you have my resume, you can see that I exceeded my employers' standards for accuracy. I was careful to follow the different payment procedures for my two employers—every finance department is a little different.

NICK: And you're working now at BuyCorp?

ANGELA: You probably know that BuyCorp has had some troubles lately. I took a severance package three weeks ago. I was sorry to leave BuyCorp, because it was a great place to work and I was allowed to help other departments in unexpected ways. Still, sales were down and some of us had to move on. Since SellCorp is adding people, I assume you're doing okay—is that a fair assumption?

NICK: We're doing great . . . let me tell you about the job's responsibilities. . . .

[The job sounds great—just what Angela is looking for. She takes the initiative.]

ANGELA: This position sounds ideal for a responsible, self-starting accountant. The minute we end this call I'm going to go online and learn more about BuyCorp, but I don't want to keep you too long. I'm certainly interested in the job, and it sounds like you are interested in talking further, so . . . when may I come in?

NICK: We're talking to several candidates, and we don't know exactly how many we will interview, so we'll call you.

ANGELA: Okay. Why don't I follow up in a few days? You have my contact information on my resume; may I have your phone number and e-mail address?

NICK: Yes.

• • •

Angela passes her phone-screening interview with flying colors. She impresses Nick with her key messages (she's accurate, follows the rules, and is helpful to other departments—all especially valuable in her profession). She returns the company's interest right away and gives a brief, candid explanation for why she's looking for a new job. Even though the recruiter didn't commit to an interview date in this call, Angela got permission to follow up. She's on her way to the next step, which is a face-to-face meeting.

Like Angela, you may face job interviews in unusual settings. The questions you'll be asked will be the same as those in chapters 3–8, but the settings require some special preparation and forethought. By tailoring your approach to the format, you move from being a good candidate to being a great one.

## Phone Interviews

The phone can ring at any time with the promise of a job at the other end of the line—so be ready to handle the call. The interviewer won't offer you a job yet; their purpose is to screen you into or out of the face-to-face interviews that finalists get. They are calling others like you—three or four candidates an hour! Here's the challenge: How do you distinguish yourself over the phone in about ten minutes? How do you make a good impression without that firm handshake or winning smile?

You must focus on your strongest selling points while projecting a superprofessional demeanor:

- Stand up and smile. Your energy and expression actually change how your voice sounds.
- Turn away from distractions and give the interviewer your full attention. Leave the room if you have to.
- Answer questions precisely and briefly.
- Don't launch into a full-blown "sales pitch" right away but make your points as you answer questions. In the example above, Angela puts her best sales points into an answer about her experience.
- Don't rush. Some people talk faster over the phone than in conversation, which can make them sound panicky.
- Promise to follow up. Get a name and phone number. If they say, "We'll call you," say thank you, find out when they'll call, and promise to follow up anyway.

For phone interviews, just a little rehearsal will launch you past the majority of candidates, so if you haven't used any of the rehearsal tactics described in chapter 2, try this: ask a friend to call you at an unexpected time with questions from chapters 3–5 of this book. Can you answer questions confidently at a moment's notice?

If you are called on a cell phone and you are unable to find a quiet place to talk, explain the situation and then set a definite time to talk, even if it's just a few minutes later. Don't interview for a job while driving in heavy traffic with two teenagers and a barking dog!

Occasionally a phone call will dive deeper than a typical screening interview, which poses a dilemma: you must cooperate, but you don't want to give away so much information that they skip a face-to-face meeting. Offer enough information to intrigue the caller *and* hint at an even deeper level of detail. For example, in response to a question like, "Tell me how you can prove your skill in PowerPoint," you can say, "My boss says I'm the most skilled at PowerPoint in the entire company. In fact, other managers ask her for my time to review their presentations. I'd be happy to show you a sample set of before-and-after slides, with confidential information removed. Would you like me to bring those in?"

If they decline to schedule a follow-up, you can also offer to add material to your resume, like this: "You know, the proof of PowerPoint skills is in the execution. Would you like to send me a presentation and see how I can improve it?" Again, your goal is to stand out among the interviewer's twenty calls that day.

## Online Interviews

Online interviews, automated entirely on the Web, are essentially sophisticated questionnaires that screen candidates in or out for a face-to-face interview. They cannot replace the human side of the interview, but they save everyone time by focusing on the "must-have" qualifications for a position.

Glen Goodman, vice president of Talent Acquisition of Centex Title, Mortgage and Insurance Group, explains: "An online application asks you questions about your customer service, your integrity level, and your selling skills. There's also simple fact-finding: what hours you're willing to work, the flexibility of your schedule, are you eligible to work in the United States, etc. This way, hiring managers talk only to those who are truly qualified. The application also gives you a gut feeling for the job. Online assessment can never replace the human process, but it saves a tremendous amount of effort and energy on everybody's part. It gives the recruiter more time to focus on the candidates who look like a fit."

Online interviews are rapidly becoming better, and employers are beginning to venture beyond the simple screening questions. Who are you as a person? Are you a cultural fit with the company? As usual, the more advanced the position, the more rigorous the interview; some companies require management candidates to go through more than an hour of online Q&A simply as a first step.

To maximize your chances of turning an online interview into a face-to-face meeting, do the following:

- Study the company's Web site before taking an online assessment—you'll pick up clues for good answers.
- Unlike phone interviews, you have as much time as you need to answer questions completely, so don't rush through the interview.
- Wherever possible, write work accomplishments into the form. "Increased sales by 15 percent" stands out when they screen your response.
- Stick to the facts; save your warm and exciting style for the face-to-face meeting.

In such a structured format, it can be tempting to bend the facts somewhat toward what you think the employer wants to hear, but don't say you can work nights when you cannot just to get a face-to-face interview—what you'll get is an annoyed manager and a reputation as a time waster.

## My Best Advice

Online interviews ask for a lot of information, and it's all relevant in ways you might not know, so do not skip any questions. Everything you answer, from your willingness to work nights to your customer service skills, is relevant to our next decision—whether to have a face-to-face interview.

—*Frank Wittenauer of professional services firm Deloitte Touche Tohmatsu*

## Video Interviews

The video interview is like a Hollywood screen test. Not only do you have to perform for the interviewer, but for the camera as well. You might be recorded speaking with your interviewer alone, or you might join an interviewer in a room with several others participating via videoconference. Perhaps you'll be directed to a local studio that provides teleconference services. Video is typically used to save money, or time, or to get many far-flung parties together. Rather than fly to company headquarters, you are seated in a small room, with a camera and monitor the size of a large television set. You see the interviewers on a screen; they see you. Depending on the technical setup, the conversation might seem a little out of sync, like talking to someone on a bad cell-phone connection.

Since this is theater, stage-manage it: A little small talk about the unique format sets everyone at ease. Ask about the location of the interviewer—if they are overseas, your time difference might be substantial. Ask if there are others in the interview you cannot see, and find out their names and job functions.

- Look and speak directly into the camera lens (it helps to imagine you are looking "through" the camera at the person).
- Don't shuffle notes, tap your foot, gesture broadly, or move around the room. These ordinary habits are distracting on a screen.
- Pause a moment before speaking. This can smooth out the slight delays that sometimes hamper a videoconference.
- If at all possible, practice in advance by answering interview questions while facing a home video camera. A few minutes of rehearsal can reduce the camera's intimidation factor.

Carole Martin, author of *Boost Your Interview IQ*, adds two technical tips for videoconferences:

- Speak up if you're experiencing any difficulty with sound, delays, or picture. This is not a time to suffer in silence. It will not be held against you if the technology is not working in your favor.

- Dress conservatively in solid colors. Keep distractions like jewelry to a minimum. Choose soft, neutral shades rather than black and white, which are too extreme on camera. Various shades of blue work well. Watch TV presenters and newscasters for other ideas about camera-ready clothes.

A tape of your interview might be replayed later for others in the hiring loop, so look your best and keep your answers short (long answers are problematic any time; on video they're slow torture, and the fast-forward button is available to zap you right out of the running).

## Traveling Interviews

Your entire interview process might take place a long way from home. This is common for overseas employment, and happens a lot in this country as well, especially for more senior positions.

If you're traveling to interview for a job, you'll have multiple interviews, so study the section below on multiple interviews carefully. Preplanning and follow-up are doubly important in the long-distance situation.

- Get a schedule ahead of time. Ask for details about everyone you'll meet (this can be done over the phone with your contact at the employer).
- Bring a change of outfit(s) if the interviews might continue over several days.
- Follow up with everyone you meet and do it the moment you get home—drop each person a thank-you note. Then follow up a second time a week later. A candidate who is physically far away feels less connected to employers during the hiring process, so you need to keep reminding interviewers of your time with them.
- Think carefully in advance about your ability to move—where you're willing to live, how much it will cost, and personal considerations such as children's school situations.[5]

---

[5] You can learn all about these issues at **monstermoving.com**.

If you are carrying luggage on the day of the interview, arrive extra early and ask for a place to store your bags. You don't want to schlep a suitcase all over HQ, dropping a bag every time someone shakes your hand!

Employers are expected to pay the cost of your travel if they have invited you to the traveling interview. (Incidentally, employers use phone, online, and videoconference interviews precisely to avoid this expense.)

## "Momentum" Interviews—Multiple Interviews

You might have many interviews in one day, or you might have a series of interviews stretching out over several days. I like to call these multiple face-to-face meetings "momentum interviews," because you're building momentum through the process. It's more a marathon than a sprint: Your first interview gets you to the 5-mile mark, and then it's all about getting to the next milestone. You can ask, "Tell me what you need to know about me to move this process forward." Then focus the conversation on that topic. At mile 10, check in with the same question. At mile 15, your mental toughness starts to waver ("How many interviews do these people need, anyway?!?") but remember: Each new interview is a good sign. They're still interested. They're *more* interested, so let that positive feedback power you to the end.

Like a marathon, momentum interviews call for the same detailed preparation as a shorter process—but more of it. You want to give the same key messages to each interviewer *and* tailor your presentation a little bit for each individual. Imagine an 80/20 ratio: 80 percent of your presentation should be consistent with each interviewer—it will be your go-to stuff—and 20 percent should be fresh material that addresses the immediate concerns of the interviewer. An intriguing candidate spices up a consistent message with a variety of examples. Prepare questions covering each individual's area of expertise.

During second, third, or fourth interviews, you have two key advantages: you know they are highly interested, and you have information from the first interview to discuss. Bring your notes and say, "Christina Rodriguez told me a little about the restructuring of the department. I wonder how you think it will affect the requirements of this job. . . ."

After a series of momentum interviews, your interviewers will share their impressions with each other, and that's when the power of your preparation carries you over the finish line. Each can say, "Hey, he gave me additional examples of the same skill." In effect, they're convincing each other to hire you.

Prepare a couple of achievement stories for each interviewer—as many as eight or ten stories. Ask for names of interviewers in advance; and learn something about each. Use each interview to build a more complete picture of the organization. ("I'll be talking to Jane Smith next . . . can you tell me how her department interacts with yours?")

## Marathon Day

You should be told in advance that you will have several interviews in one day. Prepare physically for that marathon: Bring bottled water, double up on the deodorant, and stash a small toothbrush kit in your bag or briefcase. Keep a checklist of achievement stories for a quick reminder between interviews, and carry additional resumes.

Momentum interviews reveal cultural clues, so take a moment between interviews to gather your thoughts about the organization. Have you learned more about the employer's values, priorities, and power centers? Will the job have built-in conflicts? Have you met your boss-to-be? (If not, ask why—this can be a bad sign.) How do people in the hallways dress, speak, and act? Is this your kind of place?

At a high level, some employers stage-manage multiple interviews in advance. There's the traditional good cop–bad cop routine, in which one interviewer is very friendly and persuasive, and the other is openly skeptical (treat both with respect, warmth, and caution). There's also the hidden test, as Lisa Cornay-Albright of Microsoft describes:

> Sometimes a person in the interview loop will ask a senior candidate to do something that would really be more appropriate to a junior individual . . . and the candidate gets irritated and disengages, saying, "I've been in software for twenty years. I'm not going to write a rudimentary coding exercise on the white board for you!" They don't re-

alize that the exercise is not about writing code but about justifying and communicating your ideas. They're offended, and they're going to blow the entire rest of the day.

A common question in a momentum session will ask who else you have interviewed with. Keep a list close so you don't get frustrated—or just remember! First names work fine—"I met with Bob in HR at 9, Susan and John together at 10. . . ."

A full-day marathon can include a meal, so watch your table manners! This is not a joke: I have seen top managers unconsciously talk with full mouths, push food with their fingers, and speak rudely to waiters. These turnoffs can kill an entire day of good impressions. Eat something simple (you don't want sauce on your tie or blouse), and even if alcohol is offered, candidates are better off declining a drink on interview day. Stay sharp, and save the toast for the day they offer you a job!

Momentum can take a long time to build. You might interview several times over weeks, or even months. This is especially true of executive positions. If this happens, review your previous conversations at the beginning of each interview. The burden's on you to rev up the momentum each time. Study your notes before you go in for second or third interviews so your fresh information builds additional arguments in your favor.

### Face the Jury

The panel interview tests your performance and your mettle. You face many interviewers at the same time—maybe at lunch (okay), or maybe in a windowless conference room (yikes!). Styles vary a lot—you might be peppered with unconnected questions or you might be asked to discuss one experience in excruciating detail. Take a tip from a lawyer facing the jury: Answer the individual and the group at the same time. Make eye contact with everyone—especially that quiet one farthest away (she's taking mental notes). Plunge in and try to enjoy the experience, because if a company likes panel interviews, they put a premium on teamwork! If you're feeling confident in a panel interview, you might want to take a bit of an arbitrator role as well. Act as if you're already a member of the team, like this:

*That's an interesting dilemma, Sharon. Before I tell you how I'd solve that problem, let me ask if the budget priorities Skip mentioned a moment ago apply to this department as well, or if your priorities are different . . . ? They're the same? Fine, then is it safe to assume you cannot add even temporary staff unless you can demonstrate they'll increase revenue? In that case, here's where I'd start. . . ."*

Like any marathon, momentum interviews require training, so practice those key messages! Your mental attitude, as well as patience and perseverance, are key to victory. Keep up a steady stream of follow-ups with each individual in the days following any momentum interview, even if you have one central contact at the company.

## Job Fairs

At a job fair, you might meet with a dozen potential employers for just a few minutes each. And you are trying to make an impression in a situation in which hundreds of other candidates are also present. In order to make the most out of this type of event, it is really important to prepare well (and if you've done a little homework you'll stand out—candidates at job fairs are notoriously unprepared to make a strong impression).

Before you go:

- Find out from the fair organizers which employers will be there.
- Research their Web sites; if they have a job opening that's right for you, study it and note the name or number of the job.
- Dress up, arrive on time, and bring at least twenty copies of your resume. Despite their informal atmosphere, you should appear as professional as if you were meeting with the president of a company.

At the job fair:

- Get a map. Employers will be located at individual tables or booths; head for the companies you've targeted. Time is at a premium in this setting, so don't waste it standing in line at the wrong booth.

- Focus on generating leads, not on clinching the deal. Interviewers do not have time for a 30-minute conversation. Introduce yourself, present your resume, make your key sales points, and ask to follow up, like this:

   *Hi, I'm Tasha Adams, and here is my resume. You'll see that, after two summer internships at Springfield Memorial Hospital I've had a good look at the work of a benefits administrator. I'm especially interested in Wilde Healthcare systems because of your high customer satisfaction rating in the last J.D. Power survey. Who may I talk with today about the skills I could bring to Wilde?*

If they're interested, they'll ask some standardized questions. Answer succinctly. Show enthusiasm, interest, energy. Just being friendly and composed in such a hurried setting sends a good message.

Refer to open jobs your research turned up. If you discuss specific job openings, find out how to apply then and there. Eventually you'll have to talk to the hiring manager (who often is not at the fair), so get a business card, or at least a name, for your follow-up. Because employers use job fairs to find candidates for many openings, your follow-up makes the difference between a fantasy and a face-to-face interview. So use the follow-up tactics in chapter 14 to clinch the interview.

## What Were They Thinking?

*Candidate:* "The reason I chose this company? Actually, I was rejected two weeks ago by your largest competitor, and I thought this would be my second-best option."
   —*sent to Monster's message boards by an anonymous recruiter*

**W**hat did you think of this one, Stu?" asked Melinda, passing him a resume.

"Diane Szz—Syzin . . . "

"Sosinski, Stu. S-O-S-I-N-S-K-I. It's on her resume."

"Right; Sosinski. She's cool, I guess. Something tells me she's about to have kids, though. That would be a drag."

Melinda, the SVP of Recruiting, looked at Stu over her glasses and said, "Stu, you didn't ask her about that, did you?"

"No. When I mentioned my kids she asked a lot of questions, though." He shifted in his chair, smirked, and said, "She wasn't wearing a wedding ring, though. Maybe she's gay or can't have kids or something." Melinda glared. "Hey, how would I know?" he finished.

Okay, maybe we dodged that bullet, thought Melinda. "How about the guy you talked to yesterday—the one who went by his initials?" she asked.

"A. D. Shirta or something, yeah. Indian guy. Or from Pakistan maybe . . . one of those. Now he was really smart. Knew his way around the plant; he cut his teeth at a refinery in the Gulf."

"Of Mexico?"

"No, no—the Persian Gulf. Jeez." Stu frowned at Melinda, and said, "They import all their engineers from India. Or Pakistan. Anyway, he was great but we can't get him."

"What's wrong?"

"Well, he told me he won't be a citizen until he gets married, and you won't give him a work visa or whatever."

"Did you ask him if he was a citizen?"

"No, I just asked if he was married."

Melinda stared. "You asked him if he was *married?*"

"Yes, of course. That's how they get their green cards." Stu saw he'd made a mistake. "Oh, come on, Mindy!" he said. "Everybody knows that's how they get to work here."

Melinda began to put her hand over her mouth, caught herself, and thoughtfully tapped her chin. Now it's a race, she thought, between my teaching this guy what he can and can't say, and someone tagging us with a lawsuit. . . .

• • •

Sooner or later, you're going to be asked personal questions. They might be uncomfortable, inappropriate, or illegal. You won't have time to determine the exact legal status of a question, and most of the time you'll be tempted to answer. Your answer, however, can sidetrack or even stop your momentum. Now we're talking about a serious dilemma: you could hurt your chances whatever you say.

The maddening thing about inappropriate questions is, they often seem "sort of okay" because they're related to legitimate questions. They're not usually asked with malicious intent. Stu, above, is truly ignorant of the law, and from his point of view, he's just trying to get relevant information.

Furthermore, employment laws vary from state to state. Generally, information regarding your age, marital status, country of origin, religion, sexual preference, parental status, disabilities, and/or health status is not appropriate in a job interview. An employer is permitted to ask questions related directly in the job, but experienced interviewers ask such questions indirectly.

For example, an interviewer might ask a person who uses a wheelchair, "Now that I have described the job, do you feel capable of performing the essential functions of this job with or without reasonable accommodations?" They can't ask, "Why are you in that wheelchair? Can you do the job in that?"

Some questions and comments, while not strictly discriminatory, are inappropriate. It's not an employer's business how much money your parents make or whether your kids are in private school. It's not professional for a person to comment on your appearance or table manners (even if you give them reason to do so). It's certainly inappropriate (and possibly illegal) for them to ask you out on a date. When these borderline questions are asked in small talk, your best bet is to redirect the conversation. This is another reason to be well prepared. If you are confident in your potential and presentation, you won't get thrown off-course by inappropriate questions.

You do not have to answer inappropriate questions, but unless the question is outrageous, you don't want to turn the interview into a seminar on employment law. So what do you say?

One tactic negotiation experts use in such a tense situation is to assume the interviewer means no harm and in fact, most of the time, they've strayed over the line thoughtlessly. You can defuse such questions by using one of several replies:

- **Clarify the underlying issue.** "Are you asking about my birthplace because you're concerned about my work status?"
- **Gently give them a chance to back down.** "You know, I've got a great life at home, but if you don't mind, I'd like to use the time we have to talk about this terrific job."
- **Question the question.** "That's quite a direct question. Can you tell me why you ask? Are you concerned that my religious practice will affect my performance?"
- **Redirect the question.** "Well, yes, it's certainly a hot political season here in California. How do you think a change in the government would affect your organization?"
- **Don't answer.** "Hmmmm . . . you know, I think my last direct-marketing campaign is really relevant to this job. May I tell you about that?"
- **Say no.** "No. I would rather you not call me for social reasons."

Your attitude will carry you through most of these troublesome moments. You don't want to look like a legalistic stiff, but you also don't want to give up your right to privacy. Privately, treat the question as part of your information-gathering conversation. What does it say about the employer or interviewer? Can you talk later to the HR director about the matter?

Below are some typically "questionable" questions, followed by alternative phrasings that are more acceptable. In the case of the alternatives, a direct, focused answer is your best response.

**How old are you? What is your birth date?**
Alternative:
**Are you over the age of eighteen?**

**Does your religion prohibit you from working certain days?**
Alternative:
**We sometimes work evenings, weekends, and holidays. Will this be a problem for you?**

**What country are you from? What kind of accent is that?**
Alternative:
**An ability to speak French or Spanish fluently would be a big plus in this job. Do you know either?**

**Are you a citizen of the United States?**
Alternative:
**Do you possess authorization to work for an employer in the United States?**

**How's your health? How many sick days did you take last year?**
Alternative:
**Can you safely lift this 60-pound box and stack it on this shelf four feet high? (This must be part of the job's reasonable requirements.)**

**Do you live with anyone else?**
Alternative:
**What is your contact address and phone number? (Candidates may give a mailbox address if reluctant to release a home address.)**

I love the Knights of Columbus. What clubs or social organizations do you belong to?
    Alternative:
Do you belong to any professional organizations relevant to this job?

How would your spouse feel about your traveling or relocating?
    Alternative:
Will you travel, relocate, or work overtime if necessary?

Have you ever been arrested?
    Alternative:
Have you ever been convicted of this crime: [crime relevant to the position, e.g., identity theft, for a position dealing with customer credit information]?

Do you use drugs?
    Alternative:
If we make you an offer, this job requires a confidential test for illegal drug use. Will you be willing to undergo that test?

## My Best Advice

An employer's concerns behind personal-but-legal questions should be relevant to the job's requirements and performance. As an example, if you have been convicted of embezzlement, you will probably not be considered for a job handling money. The assumption is that you had a problem in your past that could be a problem again.

Fundamentally, the interviewer wants to know if you can report to work and do the job. Any information that could be enlightening is important, but the interviewer's questions should focus on the job and your qualifications to do it.

—*Carole Martin, author of* Perfect Phrases for the Perfect Interview

Now, I'm sorry this is necessary, but I have to address a fantasy one or two readers might have: if you're asked an inappropriate question, don't think you've hit the easy road to a fat legal settlement. Criminal liability usually requires establishing a motive or intent to discriminate, which must be determined by a court of law. Discrimination lawsuits are long, expensive, murky, and cruelly fought. If you have good reason to believe your rights have been violated, by all means seek the advice of a competent attorney . . . but don't believe someone who tells you it's an easy road to riches. The price of seeking justice can be very high, and a person who prevails in a discrimination lawsuit might be labeled, fairly or not, as a potential risk by future employers.

## What Were They Thinking?

**A** woman sat down for a highly responsible position at Monster, and the first words out of her mouth were "I just got back from the doctor. I'm glad the results were negative."

About five minutes into the interview, she kicked off her shoes and started rubbing her feet together, presumably to satisfy an itch.

She didn't get the job.

—*Monster VP of Content Dan Miller*

"Do you have any questions?" asked Kevin. This was his favorite type of candidate—informed, curious, and a little assertive.

"Yes," replied Cynthia. "I'm very comfortable with the day-to-day responsibilities of the position. So far, we have not talked about metrics—how success in this job will be measured."

"Well, as a Human Resources recruiter specializing in sales, you'll be expected to fill thirty to fifty positions a year. Do you think you can do that?"

"Sure," Cynthia said quickly. Then she added, "I'm curious to know how much of your hiring is done by internal referral. How many salespeople are brought in by other salespeople?"

"Um, that's about four or five a year," said Kevin.

"I believe you could do much better than that with a really good employee referral reward program, but doing that would require a real understanding of how referral programs work. I know how they work. Would you consider managing a project like that going beyond the job description?"

"Wow. That would be great," said Kevin. "Tell me how you'd do that and still get your job done."

"Well, now that I know you're interested, let's see how you might do it with your existing Web team," Cynthia said.

**159**

The questions you ask are as important as the questions you answer. They demonstrate professional curiosity, ability to think on your feet, and commitment to finding the right job.

Your interviewer will expect routine questions ("What are office hours here?") and ask them if you must, but really, you can be much more impressive than that. Great questions prove superior investigative skills, intelligence, insight, and understanding of the job. Interesting questions are a compliment to the interviewer. The right questions leave your interviewer thinking, "Wow, if she asks questions like this before she's hired, think of what she'll be like when she's been here six months!"

In the example above, Cynthia asked one question about how success in her recruiting job would be measured, and then moved her inquiry over to a strength of hers: employee referral programs. Her question not only gave her important information about the job, it enabled her to move the conversation to another of her selling points.

Tactically, you can also use questions to set up achievement stories. "I imagine that the person you hire will be expected to redesign your customer fulfillment process, is that correct?" When they answer yes, you continue: "I have experience with that. Let me tell you about a time when I had to re-engineer a customer fulfillment function on the fly. . . ." Rehearse this tactic around your best achievement stories, in case you have not had an opportunity to tell them.

So much for making a good impression; you also must use questions to determine whether you want to work in that particular job or organization. No matter how carefully you've selected the job, there are so many factors that will cause your work to be happy or miserable that you are obliged to find out everything you can. Questions about working conditions, expectations, and culture help control your impulse to jump into the wrong position just to land a job.

Your turn to ask questions is also an opportunity to air your concerns. This is a fine balancing act; you don't want to appear negative or overly concerned at an early stage in the interview process. You don't want to divulge personal information, such as "I have a physical therapy session three times a week," unless it is directly related to your job performance. The best attitude you can take is "I just want to confirm important facts" and leave it at that.

It's not just questions you ask, but also *how* you ask them that is critical. Here's a quick list of dos and don'ts about the way to ask questions:

DO:
- Ask "who, what, when, where, why, and how" questions that require a certain amount of elaboration—not just yes or no—to answer. This stimulates conversation.
- Share positive information about yourself while asking questions. For example: "My media presentation skills have been praised in every performance review. Will I have opportunities to talk directly to the press in this job's capacity?"
- Ask tough questions, but do it with a smile. You can ask difficult or even awkward questions without being confrontational.
- Show enthusiasm! You are asking questions because you're seriously considering this job.
- Watch your timing. "Any questions?" is not an invitation for a hour-long cross-examination (unless they pick up the conversation by asking you more questions).

DON'T:
- Reject the answer. Mentally note new information and be alert to evasive or ignorant answers (sometimes the interviewer might be too embarrassed to admit he doesn't know the answer).
- Ask about salary, stock options, vacation, holiday schedule, or benefits unless the interviewer specifically brings it up. Ask too early, and they'll think you're more interested in the money or benefits than the job itself. Save an in-depth discussion of these issues for the last interview, or after they make an offer.
- Ask questions that have already been answered in the interview, just for the sake of asking something.
- Get personal beyond small talk. It might not be illegal for you to ask the interviewer if she's married, but it sure is inappropriate!

Carole Martin, author of *Perfect Phrases for the Perfect Interview,* suggests you consider where your interviewer sits in the process. Your questions should go to matters near and dear to the heart (or at least the job) of the interviewer:

- For HR managers and recruiters: Ask about the company and the department.
- For a hiring manager (your future boss): Ask about the job, the department, the team, and the challenges.
- For senior management: They've probably established you're qualified for the job, so ask about strategy, industry trends, and the big challenges. You can also ask them (as well as confident managers) big, audacious questions of the type found on pages 168–70.
- For other employees: Cultural questions, depending on your level of rapport with the individual, may be asked of anyone. A referral or peer-level employee of the company will often give you a more candid answer than someone trying to "sell" you the job.
- Informational interviewers: Outside the job interview context, these are the people you'll encounter in your job networking. You want to ask questions that help them direct you to job possibilities, employers, or other networking contacts.

## Questions to Ask HR or Recruiters

### Is there anything else you need to know about my ability to do this job?

This is a springboard to discussing skills they haven't mentioned yet. Extra points for mentioning a critical point from your research: "Your last press release stressed your commitment to the small-business sector. May I tell you about my experience generating small-business leads?"

## Why is this position open?

Ask gently—you're curious to know. If they tell you someone was promoted, ask what about their performance was outstanding enough to deserve the promotion. If someone was fired, and the interviewer does not say why, let it rest for the moment (but if it seems important, you should ask the manager later, when you know they are interested in you).

## Is success in this job measurable? What are those metrics?

It is absolutely crucial to get any quantifiable standards for job performance out on the table before you accept a job. The answer will tell you a lot about the organization's management and performance review style, which might range from tightly controlling to "gut feel" reviews. (Warning: If they grade on gut feel alone, consider what might happen if a new manager comes in who just doesn't like you.)

## Where do you anticipate a high performer in this job would advance?

Candidates are shy about asking this question, but I think it shows good qualities like ambition, foresight, and commitment to a great career. Don't get into a situation where your chances for promotion depend on whether your manager gets fired or dies!

## When will you select a final candidate?

There's a subtle message here: I'm in control of my job search and I'm working on other possibilities. You'll likely get an answer like "Well, we're seeing a lot of candidates and we hope to find someone as soon as possible." In that case, say thanks and ask the next question.

## When and how may I follow up?

Suggest a method for follow-up, either e-mail, letter, or phone call. See chapter 14 for a full discussion of follow-up. This is also the moment to offer to send additional materials. For example, a candidate for a marketing job might follow up with a packet of marketing materials she created.

### Why do you like working here?

If you are relaxed and confident enough to ask the HR director this personal-but-professional question, expect a surprised smile. Their answer will contain important cultural clues about working conditions, how employees are valued, and how the company mission is realized. Want to really knock them out? Ask this question the way a sophisticated interviewer would ask: "Tell me why you would decline an offer to work at another company."

### What's the compensation? What benefits, incentives, etc., does the organization offer for this job?

Stop! You should ask compensation questions only if it is late in the process. Wait for the employer to volunteer this information at the time of the offer. If you suspect the money won't be in your expected range—a ticklish situation during the interview—handle the matter indirectly, as in this phone conversation between second and third interviews: "Thanks for asking me back. We've spoken twice, and I'm gratified that you think I'd be a good member of this team. You should know I'm very interested. As we set up this third meeting, perhaps it's time to confirm the general compensation range for this job."

## Questions to Ask Managers

### What are this position's first and second priorities?

Priorities are about outcomes, not written job functions. If the manager talks about responsibilities and tasks, ask carefully what those functions will accomplish in the big scheme of things. You're looking for clues that reveal the reality of day-to-day work. For example, the job might include preparing meals, but the priority might be offering the best meals with the least spoilage or wasted effort.

## What, specifically, will this position be expected to accomplish in the next three months? The next six months?

Another check on outcomes versus responsibilities. Too many candidates join a company thinking about daily tasks without a clear set of goals, milestones, and accomplishments. This question alone can turn an ordinary interview into a very lively, upbeat conversation, as the manager gets a chance to imagine all the glorious things you'll accomplish together.

## Do you have a set of procedures to achieve this goal? If an employee comes up with an improvement, how would it be implemented?

First days on the job usually include an orientation to "how we do things around here." Better to know in advance what procedures you'll be expected to follow, if only to help you hit the ground running. The willingness and interest in improvement—or lack of it— will tell you boatloads about your prospective manager's style.

## What is this job's authority to spend money/manage people/otherwise use company resources?

Do you get a clear answer or a vague, elusive one? Measure the information carefully against their performance expectations. This can lead to an in-depth discussion of just how you'll accomplish that miracle in six months without staff or budget! Your authority might be proportional to their opinion of you, so dig deep on this one.

## If you had to off-load one of your responsibilities to someone in this position, what would it be?

A business question, but also a personal one. How does the manager react? Does he or she have something in mind for the future of this job? It's a nice opening to build rapport, as the manager thinks, "Hmmm . . . I wonder if this person could take that responsibility I never have time for. . . ."

## What's your preferred form of communicating/ managing/giving feedback to your direct reports?

This and similar questions open up the conversation to the manager's preferred style. Does it fit with yours? Will you prosper with a hands-on micromanager or a looser style?

## Describe the best employee you've ever managed. What made them great? Where are they now?

First, it's a chance for the manager to reflect on a pleasant experience. Second, no other question will tell you more about what the manager values in an employee. Now, aren't you glad you asked?

## My research says you beat your competition on price. How do you keep your costs down? Can you sustain that advantage?

You're not really confirming your research; you're showing them you've done your homework. This demonstrates respect, intelligence, and a grasp of the big picture. It also turns the interview from an interrogation to a conversation among colleagues.

Note: They may decline to answer specifically, citing confidential information—but you can still win by citing your accomplishments. For example: "Let me tell you how I hold down costs in my current job. . . ."

## My Best Advice

This isn't really rocket science. You do some research on the company, and come up with questions. However, a lot of people just look at a book [like this one] and ask questions randomly. If those questions are not relevant to you and the job, it's obvious you don't really care. Here's a bit of radical advice: ask questions in which you care about the answers.

—Mark Bidwell, Automatic Data Processing Inc.

## Cultural Questions

### Tell me something important about the company culture I wouldn't know unless I worked here for six months.

A reversal of the question on page 83, this question will take most interviewers by surprise—and you can expect a positive comment (no interviewer will say, "You'll find out that the mission statement is a lie."). This is an opener to talk about the ties between your personal culture and the organization's.

### How are employee achievements recognized?

Money, prestige, advancement, perks? Every organization is different. You want to know not just *how* achievement is recognized but also *why*. This is key evidence of the company's values. Everyone says "People are our number-one priority!" and not many really walk the talk.

(I knew a small company whose unofficial employee slogan was "We do our jobs well, and the reward for that is, we get to keep our jobs." If you won't settle for that kind of workplace, you're my kind of candidate.)

### Please comment on how the company's stated mission and values are put into effect in day-to-day work.

Like the previous question, this is also a reality check. Give the interviewer a chance to prove that the mission and values statements in the lobby are the real thing.

### Does this organization participate in sponsorships, philanthropy, or volunteer projects?

Okay, you've asked tough questions, so here's an easy one to build rapport, and the follow-up is also easy: "Why?" If you already know the answer from your research, focus on one point: "I see employees are encouraged to volunteer for the Boys and Girls Club events. How many participate?"

### Other than performing your job well, what does it take to succeed here?

This is partly about personal culture. Most organizations favor an "ABC Co. type of person" who shares their values and style. Frankly, it's also about office politics. A sharp candidate scopes out office politics before accepting an offer, but very few interviewers will discuss the subject. (Ironically, office politics is one of the first things peers reveal to new employees!) You can find a way through this maze by asking indirect, positive questions like this one. Then, network with trusted insiders—or *ex*-employees—to get other points of view!

## Big, Audacious Questions— For Confident Candidates Only!

Ask these as your momentum builds in second or third interviews, or as clarifying questions after an offer is made. Be careful to project enthusiasm for the job as you ask: "This is an important decision and I want to make sure we cover everything as I make a commitment to the job."

## What is this job's most frustrating challenge?

Depending on the answer, this might inform you about the job and the company culture. Discussion to follow: What am I expected to do to overcome the frustration (or is that just an accepted part of the job)? It's a good way to know if the job will test your skills or your tolerance for frustration.

## What's your biggest concern about this department? This job?

Want to show confidence? Ask this question of the executive to whom your prospective manager reports. You're not asking them to betray the manager's trust; you're learning if you're boss-to-be and *his* boss tell a consistent story.

## What are your plans for expansion and how would I fit into such an expansion?

Demonstrate that you are thinking not just about the job but the future. Employers respect someone who takes an active, planning role in his or her growth.

## Can you give me an example of how the company handles work–life issues?

You may address this if they express a specific concern about your family or outside life. You should not reveal private information (see chapter 10).

Usually, this question is better put as a follow-up after an offer is made, for example: "I have a long-term family commitment that requires me to leave work at 4:30 every Wednesday. Of course I'll come in early that day. I assume that won't be a problem?"

## How do I stack up against other candidates you've seen?

Why not scope out the competition? You must project confidence when you ask, or you will appear to be either (a) so insecure they'll doubt your abilities, or (b) so desperate they'll lowball the salary offer.

### Under what circumstances would this company put its preferred culture—values or principles—aside to accomplish a business goal?

You're really asking if they walk their talk, but this question carries more weight if you ask it in the context of a business dilemma, so save it for a manager or executive. Do they present a balanced view of responsibilities and aspirations? Is the company culture able to handle tough times as well as good times? Listen carefully for clues about office politics, and don't miss an opportunity to express your values about similar dilemmas.

### Please tell me about a time this department had a serious, unavoidable conflict with another department. How did you handle it?

"We never have such conflicts" is either a statement of amazing organizational alignment, or a lie. Both beg for further investigation. If your prospective manager speaks candidly about conflicts, you'll pick up lots of information that will not only help you make a good decision about the job, but also help you later, when you're doing the job.

### Every department is important, but one or two are thought of as the company's leading groups. Is this department one of those?

If you know the answer is yes, ask the line manager. If you suspect the answer is no, you might reserve this question for your networking contacts. Depending on your level of rapport with the interviewer (and their level of discretion), the discussion may range from office politics to the business plan, and this is important stuff! Be prepared to answer the counterquestion, "Why is that important to you?"

### Tell me how the CEO would describe this department to a potential large investor.

This forces your interviewer to think outside the usual frame of reference. Sure, the CEO likes the department fine, but would he or she describe it as critical, nice-to-have, or trouble? Narrowly, this is a question about status, but you can direct it back to a conversation about how the department fits into the big picture. In the case of a not-for-profit organization, you might ask how the department would be described to the organization's board of directors or trustees.

# Informational Interviews

Informational interviews are face-to-face research. They are used to generate job leads and practice your interview performance. Conducting a good informational interview requires that you prepare questions carefully.

For formal meetings (with a well-connected acquaintance, a mentor, or an employee at an organization you're targeting), treat the informational interview exactly like a job interview: Make an appointment and arrive on time. Dress professionally. Do your homework. Focus your questions on generating leads, either discovering new potential employers or getting new information about employers you're targeting.

This kind of interview might also take place spontaneously. If the person next to you on the soccer sideline is willing to discuss her employer, you don't have to change into a suit to get great information. If you've memorized a few questions, you can turn a chat into a job lead . . . and schedule a formal interview for the next week.

## *Questions for Generating Leads (After Describing Your Key Selling Points)*

- ▶ *Who do you know who might need my skills?*
- ▶ *Who do I approach at ABC Co.?*
- ▶ *Do you know anyone doing this kind of work?*
- ▶ *Who else makes this product/service?*
- ▶ *Are there industries or types of organizations where I should look that I haven't mentioned, such as nonprofit, start-up, or small business?*

## Questions That Improve Your Performance in a Job Interview

▶ *How can I be attractive to ABC Co.?*
▶ *What do they seek in a candidate?*
▶ *What's the culture like there?*
▶ *What's coming up in their business in the next year?*
▶ *Do they have hidden challenges, organizational problems, or a new competitor?*

And always, at the close of an informational interview, ask this question:

▶ *Would you be willing to introduce/refer me to someone at that organization?*

## What Were They Thinking?

When I was a school principal, we found a mannequin in a storage room. During the summer, when most of the hiring took place, I dressed the mannequin and sat it on a chair in my office. Perfectly ordinary, right?

Now you're a candidate coming in for a job. You walk into the office, and there sitting in another chair is this mannequin. How do you react? How do you respond? Do you ignore it? Do you acknowledge it? Do you ask a question or two?

It was fascinating to see how candidates dealt with that. One I remember very clearly saying, "I'm not gonna go through with this interview as long as that mannequin is here!" Not exactly ready for the stress of a high school class. Others would ask questions, and some would play along with the "joke." It told me a lot about the kind of person each candidate was.

—*Donald Weintraub, Rainmaker Associates*

# 12 Starting Out or Starting Over

**P**aula, a recruiter who specialized in hiring new graduates, interviewed five candidates in a typical day at her firm. Sam, the young man sitting in her cubicle, had passed the preliminary tests—he was dressed well, on time for the appointment, and seemed to have a good, professional attitude. Sticking to her efficient routine, Paula asked the first formal question—the one she always liked to ask early in an interview.

"What's your greatest strength?"

Sam acknowledged her question with a nod and began eagerly: "Well, I'm very self-motivated. I know you've probably heard that before, so let me give you an example. For the last couple of years, I've volunteered part-time at my college's computer help desk. It was a job similar to the one we're discussing, and you can see it at the top of my resume."

He continued. "I wanted experience helping people with computer-related problems, so I approached the information technology director and asked her if she'd teach me to work on the help desk in exchange for my time and efforts. It's turned out to be great for both of us. She's gotten much-needed help, and I've been able to gain hands-on experience I wouldn't have gotten otherwise."

Thank goodness, thought Paula. Someone who can talk about experience without my having to coax it out of him. He might be a keeper. . . .

Two job interview situations call for a little extra preparation on your part. If you are a student or new graduate, you will have to give a strong interview to compensate for your lack of formal job experience. If you are changing careers, you will have to help interviewers jump the conceptual gap between your old career and your new one.

In both cases, you'll be asked the same questions that appear in previous chapters. Your additional challenge is that your competition will often have more directly relevant job experience than you.

Landing an interview in the first place is a positive sign; it means the interviewer is open to hearing your case (instead of dismissing you out of hand). This is an extra consideration and you must acknowledge it by preparing that case more carefully than a more typical candidate. In other words, you have to out-hustle your competition.

## Recent Graduates

Recent graduates have to back up their claims with more than a good grade point average. In particular, you need to move quickly past clichés like "I'm a self-starter" or "I'm a people person." Interviewers have heard these lines a thousand times.

Instead, present your claims in the context of achievement stories, as Sam did in the opening of this chapter. Look at the personal qualities in his answer that prove the self-motivated claim:

- Sam volunteered to help.
- He knew he needed experience and sought it out.
- He approached the right person directly with a win-win proposition.
- He performed well in the job, providing much-needed help.

These personal qualities all promote success in a job.

Career counselor Peter Vogt observes that your school experience can even translate to hypothetical situations. For example, an interviewer asks, "You're working with a small team and you have a significant conflict with one of your team members. What would you do?" You can tell a story about a similar situation at college:

*That actually happened to me once in a social psychology course I took. We were doing a group project, and it was clear that one person wasn't doing his share of the work. I talked with other people in the group about it, and they felt the same way I did. So I offered to talk to this person about our concerns. I'm really glad I did. As it turns out, he was stressed out, because his father had been in the hospital for several weeks having tests done. He was having trouble in all of his classes. So I mentioned the fact that our school has a counseling center and encouraged him to go there. He did, and he got the help he needed. The rest of us then divided up his work.*

As a new graduate, you will be asked many variations on the question, "Why shouldn't I hire someone more experienced?" Do not see this as a hostile question! See it as an invitation to convince the interviewer you possess all the qualities the job requires.

Make extra preparations to tell your achievement stories. Study chapter 6 and complete the exercise on page 3 titled, "Mastering the Freestyle Interview."

Remember: Experience counts, but experience is not limited to having performed every single task in a job description—especially early in your career. In business today, a proven ability to learn and grow counts as well. They wouldn't be talking to you if they didn't think you might be a positive addition to the company.

## Internships

Interviewing for an internship—a temporary job while you're still in school—is similar to a first-timer job interview. Before graduation, you generally have even less experience, so you need to translate your academic and work-study experience into the context of the internship. Storytelling becomes that much more important: "At my fraternity this is what I did; as a tour guide, this is how I handled an uncomfortable situation; in my job at the dining hall, this was my responsibility. . . ."

Internships typically don't pay much, but they do pay off. For example, an internship at one of the big television networks in New

York is highly coveted—and very competitive—because it typically tracks right into a job after graduation.

You'll need a solid resume, a good cover letter, and (sometimes) a transcript of your grades. You still need to hold your own with rapport and culture questions, because the interviewer is always thinking, "Would I hire this person after graduation?"

Finding a good internship begins with what you ask—the questions that you as a college sophomore ask your parents, friends, etc. Develop a list of target companies during the school year and *use your school's career center*. This is the time to begin networking as well—use connections from professors, national fraternal organizations, and school alumni to secure interviews.

## My Best Advice

**N**ew graduates can minimize their anxiety before a job interview by preparing more thoroughly than their peers. Here's a checklist of steps you must take, cued to chapters in this book:

1. **Research the Company/Organization in Depth.** Fairly or unfairly, your interviewer will expect you to know quite a bit about his organization.
2. **Identify What You Have to Sell.** What are the top three skills and experiences you can offer to the employer that other applicants can't? Can you prove them with stories? See chapters 2 and 6.
3. **Develop Some Intelligent Questions.** From chapter 11, select at least three questions you will ask the interviewer.
4. **Get Primped.** You need to look your best. Adopt the professional look and demeanor described in chapter 13.
5. **Be Ready for Surprises.** You may be invited to lunch. You may be asked to take a pre-employment test or a drug test. You may be interviewed by more than one person. An interviewer may be crabby, abrupt, or just clueless. These scenarios are described throughout the book, but the most important

preparation you can make in advance is to know that the interview process won't go perfectly. Accept this ahead of time, and you'll take some of the pressure off yourself so that you'll make fewer mistakes and omissions during the actual interview.

—*Peter Vogt, president of Career Planning Resources*

## Career Changers

You did one job for a long time, but now that type of job has disappeared. Or, you stepped out of the workforce to raise a family. Or, you've outgrown your old profession and you want to work at something more challenging in the next phase of your career. These career-changer scenarios are more and more common; most interviewers know someone who's been through it. Again, if you've gotten to the point where they're interviewing, they are probably open to your candidacy. You just have to make a more compelling case than your competition.

If you are older, you may have to overcome three myths about career changers with these responses:

**Myth:** You can't teach an old dog new tricks.
**Response:** There is a learning curve with any new employee, including anyone coming from the same job in another company. You bring a fresher point of view to a job than someone who says, "I've always done it this way." And when it comes to learning new tricks, don't forget motivation: you are deliberately seeking a new professional challenge, and are thus motivated to learn, grow, and change.

**Myth:** Career changers think entry-level jobs are beneath them.
**Response:** If you're applying for an entry-level job, you have already accepted that job's responsibilities. As a more experienced candidate, you bring a wealth of knowledge that most entry-level candidates do not possess.

**Myth:** Career changers are less loyal to their employers.

**Response:** First, loyalty is a quality of character. Second, loyalty works when both sides are getting a good deal. Third, career changers are more adaptable in rapidly changing workplaces because they have a broader range of experiences than candidates who have been in one job for a long time.

Beyond the myths, a career changer's most urgent task is to overcome the inevitable question, "Why should I hire a beginner in this field when there are candidates knocking on my door who more closely match the job?" The answer to that is, "because I'd be better in the long run, and here's the proof."

Your key tactic during the interview is to translate the skills, work habits, and judgment you acquired elsewhere to the new job. Your achievement stories bridge the gap by focusing on your strengths in three ways:

- Put translatable skills from your last job in the context of the current job. For example, if organizational skills are an important part of your next job, prepare stories from past work that emphasize your use of those skills (even if they were secondary at the time).
- Make life experience relevant to the current job. This is especially important if you left the workplace for more than five years. Bring in stories about work in the community, in children's schools, or in volunteer organizations. If the interviewer seems receptive, you can talk about complicated home management tasks like keeping a budget *if* the skills involved are truly relevant to the job.
- Detail important skills you learned since your last formal job. This is a good tactic if you left the workplace to pursue self-employment, but have now decided to return to an employer. Tell stories about the skills and self-motivation you learned out on your own. Many interviewers will admire (or even secretly envy) the person who tried to make it as an entrepreneur.

Since career changing is a growing phenomenon, many interviewers have heard all sorts of flabby stories connecting one job to another—

"I can manage a laboratory because I used to manage a call center." Your bridge must be more solid. Here's an example of a bridge that worked, from outplacement executive Colin Moor of Keystone Associates:

> A few years ago, a large corporation went out of business. Many of the new opportunities for senior managers locally were in small organizations—a big change from corporate culture. Typically, they'd pitch these small companies, saying, "Hey, even though I managed a division with four hundred people I'm really a hands-on type. . . ." It sounded false.
>
> One successful candidate, however, drew from his life outside of work, and said: "I coach sports in my community. I've worked with seven-year-olds and with thirteen-year-olds. Big companies are like the older kids. It's harder to have an impact on them. They act like they know everything. You don't seem to have much influence on them. But the seven-year-olds are like a small company. They'll listen to you, and if you meet them where they are developmentally, you'll have a big impact. . . ." He went on to use this analogy to sell the value of his teaching and mentoring skills, and all of a sudden people were listening to him. He was sincere, he made a legitimate point, and he got a great job.

Career changers should have ready answers to questions like these:

**How carefully have you considered your career change? Will you commit to it for a minimum of five years before changing again?** Briefly describe the deliberate process that brought you to make the change. Try to appear proactive—you are seeking a new horizon—instead of reactive. Interviewers are unsettled by an answer that ends with "Well, there were no more jobs in my field, so I switched." Even if economic conditions started your transition, move on quickly to describe a positive, forward-looking attitude. As for long-term commitment: you have many choices but only one life, so I assume you've chosen a new field carefully and can tell the interviewer why you've made the commitment to change. As for five years versus three years or seven years, that's a debatable point depending on economic conditions; but if the interviewer insists on a number, I assume you can say yes.

**How much do you know about this specific field and job?** If you've done your research, the first part of this question is a breeze. If you haven't . . . go back and research!

**Will you take as long to get up to speed as an entry-level candidate?** No. It will take you *less* time to get up to speed because unlike an entry-level candidate you have less to learn in terms of judgment, common sense, and good work habits.

**What specific skills or experience do you have that proves you'll outperform more traditionally qualified candidates?** To answer this question, take some time before the interview to make one-to-one comparisons between your skills and experience and the job description. It really helps to write down your answers: "The help desk job requires quick resolution of a customer's problems, and that means I'll have to be skilled at asking the right questions. I learned to ask good questions in my customer service position at a catalog company ten years ago."

**How big a stretch is this switch?** This is actually a friendly question, inviting you to make the case that it isn't such a big switch by citing all the common skills or knowledge between this job and your last. In general, you can make the case to change industries based on common skills between jobs, or you can make a case that you can change jobs within an industry. Changing both industries and job types at once is a longer process, usually requiring some additional school or at least training in new skills.

As a career changer, you are not alone! The great challenge facing employers today is how to continually adapt their employees to a changing, global economy . . . and the employee with a demonstrated taste for change has become, more and more, the person that employers want to find.

## What Were They Thinking?

**S**ome career changers just haven't thought very hard about making a case. I interviewed a gentleman for a television field technician position. His background did not reflect any type of experience in electronics or televisions. I asked him if he had ever taken off the back of a TV and actually seen the inside.

His response was this: "Are you kidding? It's dangerous back there!" Needless to say, he did not get the position.

—*Anonymous HR director*

# 13  How to Make a Great Impression

Sharon placed two pages of notes side by side on her desk. One was labeled "Phil MacNeil" and the other "Martin Green," and now it was decision time. Two candidates with almost the same experience, skills, and salary range. As always, Sharon had an intuitive liking for one more than the other; Phil seemed more polished, more professional-looking. As always, Sharon worried that her personal preferences would influence her recommendation to the hiring manager.

She circled words at the top of each page of notes:

Martin: High skill—good story re: Plant cleanup—6 yrs. current position (still there but wants to grow—no pressure to leave). *Ambivalent about job stress.*
Phil: High skill—Professional & Confident—3 mos. unemployed—knows us—knows what he wants—good questions! *OK re: stress.*

The last point, their ability to handle stress, marked the clear difference between Martin and Phil, and it was critical. The job was definitely stressful, with deadlines and performance targets applying relentless pressure. Sharon suspected that the department's leader was burning out; she was quietly beginning to look around the company for another position for him.

Phil proved he could step up to the difficult tasks: Not only had he

**182**

told several stories about hitting the goals under stress, but he'd also related his experience of closing down a failing business he'd inherited from his father-in-law. He had handled the whole ugly matter with expertise, patience, and class; he had gone to the right places for help; he'd kept the stress from affecting his family.

Sharon wasn't surprised. Phil's confidence, consideration, and respect inspired the same response in her. And that might be the most important quality he'd need in the job.

Sharon stapled her notes about Martin to his resume and placed it in a file, then picked up the phone. She was going to send Phil to the manager as the final candidate.

Until now, you've focused most of your interview preparation on the questions you'll be asked. If you've actually prepared answers to questions in chapters 3–12 (and I hope you have), you are ready to handle almost any part of the interview conversation. Before you go to the interview, though, there are two more pieces of the process to master: your presentation and your follow-up. Given that two candidates may have equally great stories to tell, and equal skill sets, the candidate who makes the strongest positive impression during and after the interview gets the job.

Now you're going to consider how to look, dress, and behave like the consummate professional your hard work has prepared you to be. Your "professional presence" ties together all the different elements of your interview preparation, and carries you through the interview process.

The good news is that, once you make that good impression, the interviewer will often give you the benefit of the doubt, and seek to reinforce that good impression. They will ask questions that lead you to distinguish yourself from other candidates. They will listen carefully to the questions you ask.

There's a chameleon quality to a person with good interview skills. A good candidate doesn't actually change her persona, but she does adjust what she chooses to highlight in an interview. Remember the 80/20 ratio. You'll always lay the foundation of your candidacy by mentioning your top skills and achievement at the appropriate moment. They prove that you have the skills, knowledge, and character to be a great member of the employer's team.

The remainder of your presentation should adjust to the specific interviewer. What are his top concerns? If he's the manager who would be your boss, his concern might be more about your ability to produce under pressure. If she's the CEO, she might be thinking more about your potential to grow into a position of leadership over time.

This is the 20 percent of the interview in which you will use additional achievement stories, personal anecdotes that reveal your strengths, and the "color commentary" about your nonwork interests. It's important to have this additional material to draw from as the interview process proceeds. If you have new stories to tell in second or third interviews, you will become a richer, more interesting person to the interviewer(s).

By the time you get to the interview, you will have prepared detailed answers to interview questions, yet you need to avoid looking too carefully scripted. People hire people, not robots, and if you mechanically insert the words "results-oriented" into every answer, you'll sound canned—like the salesman who repeats a prospect's name at the beginning of every sentence. ("Bob, I want you to know, Bob, that this product will help you. Because, Bob, I believe in your company . . . right, Bob?")

Canned answers kill the spirit of conversation because they sound like you're "spinning" the truth. You might find yourself spinning toward the door, not the job!

# The Day Before the Interview

All the mental preparation you've done can be seriously damaged by little glitches in the interview process, so take care of potential problems in advance.

## Dress the Part

You'll get a lot of advice from friends on how to dress for an interview, and I think people put a little too much faith in making their interview get-up look exactly right. Your attire, like your demeanor, won't get you the job by itself, but it sets the stage for the deeper conversation. If you dress poorly, they'll infer negatives—that you are naïve, or that you don't understand the job or company culture. Dressing well can even overcome prejudices. For example, an older candidate can dress in a stylish, contemporary outfit, which gives the impression that she's energetic and up-to-date. Likewise, an entry-level candidate in a smart, professional suit sends the message that he knows how to act in a business setting.

The simplest rule to follow: Dress in standard business attire.

**For men:** A suit and tie. Buy the best suit you can afford, and spend a few extra dollars getting it tailored. A well-fitted, well-styled suit makes you look successful. Wear good shoes—polished, please (for five bucks you can get a professional polish in hotels; sales reps will tell you it still makes a difference). A white shirt is the least risky choice, and standard blue or subtly striped shirts are okay, too. (Get your suit and shirts professionally cleaned and pressed—it makes a difference!)

Ease up on the cologne, flashy watches, attention-grabbing eyeglasses, or other jewelry (except for wedding or engagement rings). Keep your hair (and facial hair) clean and well trimmed.

**For women:** A suit with a skirt is the standard interview outfit. Skirt length varies according to fashion, so stick with whatever length is currently considered professional. Depending on fashion and a company's culture, a well-tailored pantsuit can be appropriate as well. Polish those dress shoes (no overly high heels, no open toes). Wear light jewelry, makeup, and perfume. Look to business women in your area for a simple, realistic guide to what's appropriate.

Be conservative with accessories like a purse or briefcase. In most business settings, a backpack looks silly with a suit, so carry your resumes in a portfolio or briefcase.

Many work environments became casual in the past few years, and candidates wonder if dressing in "business formal" attire is inappropriate. First, don't believe what you see on TV—an interviewer isn't interested in whether you look like a celebrity. The business-casual look might even be fine for an interview at certain companies, but I'd still advise a good sport coat or blazer, dress shirt, and tie for men, and the equivalent sport coat or blazer, blouse, and jewelry for women.

There are degrees to which you might deviate from the standard uniform, depending on the company culture and the job you seek. A more conservative look is generally appropriate for jobs in sales, finance, law, and other professions. A more relaxed look can be right for jobs in marketing, creative fields, phone service, and many technology jobs. Certain fashion-conscious industries like advertising and entertainment value a more trend-conscious look, and for that you might want to adjust. Remember: You can overcome a slightly too conservative look with your behavior, but it's hard to overcome a too-casual look, especially in a first interview.

Overt religious, political, or personal symbols in jewelry certainly tell something about the real person, but discussions about personal topics don't belong in job interviews. They're best left at home unless they're related to the job. At the least, you risk distracting the interviewer's attention. It's best to focus on the job and the fit in the early stages of the interview process, and if there are important personal matters to cover, save them for subsequent interviews.

If you regret that giraffe tattoo on your ankle, cover it discreetly. If you regret that giraffe tattoo on your neck—think of a good way to explain how it got there. Or wear a high collar!

If you really want to deviate from the standard suit, at least do it with some information. It's all right to visit the interview site in advance and study how people are dressed in the lobby. Dress as well as the best-dressed person you see.

If they really want you to dress down for the second interview, they'll tell you—and even if you go to "business casual," look a little sharper than they do. Get your khakis, shirts, and blouses down to the dry cleaner: light starch, hangers.

The day before the interview, pack your briefcase or bag with the following:

- Several clean copies of your resume.
- A copy of the cover letter or e-mail message that you have sent to this employer.

- A completed copy of the "tip sheet" at the end of this chapter, to use as a quick study before and between interviews (page 197).
- Copies of other documents such as writing samples, commendations, or awards.
- A list of references who will recommend you for the job.
- Personal business cards, with your name and contact information. If you're employed, don't hand out lots of cards bearing the name of your current employer . . . unless you want the interviewer to call you there.
- A notebook, pen, and some paper to make notes before, during, and after the interview.
- The names of the people you are meeting and the address with directions.
- Your calendar (for making follow-up appointments).
- You might also want a comb, tissues, and breath mints (not gum) for a break in the restroom.

## The Day of the Interview

Don't have something different for breakfast on the day of your interview. If you don't drink coffee, don't start today, because you'll be bouncing off walls and running to the bathroom!

- Arrive ten minutes before the interview (not an hour early; not five minutes late).
- Use the restroom before the interview (but don't be there when the interviewer comes out to get you!).
- Demonstrate that you respect the interviewer's time, and take as much of it as they will give you. It's the interviewer's job to signal a close, and you should be aware of their time restrictions.
- Be friendly and professional with everyone. The receptionist announces you; a bad first impression will be passed along to your interviewer. Be courteous to every assistant you meet. They have a vote in your job in many companies.
- Even when waiting in the lobby, project an alert and professional

persona. Candidates often run into a senior manager in front of the lobby. I make it a point to greet people in Monster's reception area even if they're not interviewing with me personally. And I'll say, "I just want to welcome you to Monster; what position are you interviewing for?" I get an impression of the candidate that I'll share later with the interviewer.

- Don't be high maintenance. A glass of water or cup of coffee is sometimes offered, but ask for nothing. Show you're ready to go "as is."

## The First Impression

It isn't fair, it isn't scientific, it isn't even smart, but it's a fact of life: a good first impression opens an interviewer's mind; a bad first impression closes it.

Do you have a firm handshake, and make good eye contact? Do you stand up straight? Are you well dressed and groomed? How do you respond to small talk? You want to set the stage for a good conversation by eliminating distractions.

Checking out another person quickly is just animal instinct. Maybe the interviewer isn't sizing you up for lunch, but in those first few moments she is definitely anticipating whether the interview is going to be enjoyable, mediocre, or downright painful. You want to inspire confidence, and get the momentum spinning you toward the job.

Here's the first-impression checklist that lurks in the back of the interviewer's mind:

✔ Candidate walks confidently into the room.

✔ Looks alert.

✔ Professionally dressed.

✔ Well groomed and neat.

✔ Clean—not too much cologne, perfume, deodorant, or smells of candy/gum/tobacco/coffee/alcohol.

- ✔ Shoes are polished and professional (no open toes, sneakers, or waffle-stompers).

- ✔ Opening words are positive and appropriate.

Get these items checked off quickly and move on to the next step.

Body language says a lot, especially when communicating feelings and attitudes. Stand up straight as the interviewer approaches. Smile. Shake hands firmly but don't crush the other person's hand. (If you actually have to practice a firm handshake, here's a tip: imagine the other person's hand is firm, yet it is also a valuable object being passed to you.) Look the interviewer in the eyes.

Stand-up comics will tell you they work hard to figure out an audience. You do the same thing at the outset. Is the interviewer friendly or formal? Interested or uninterested? Look around at things in the interviewer's office, or respond with interest to their first comments.

Small talk sets you both at ease, and good interviewers look for early clues in a quick chat. "Did you find the place all right?" (Obviously you did, so take advantage to tip them off on your thoroughness—"Yes, the directions on your Web site are helpful," or, "Actually, I took a quick run by here yesterday, just to make sure I'd get here on time and get every minute I can with you.").

Caution: Interviewers sometimes use small talk to disarm a candidate. For example, the interviewer might say, "I was up late last night trying to finish my taxes. Did you get yours in on time?" If you say, "Yeah, I always finish mine at the last minute, too," you're implying a habit—postponing unpleasant but necessary tasks—that isn't beloved in the workplace.

Take your cue from your interviewer as to how long you chat. In a short time, you'll move on to the reason you're here.

## Project a Professional Demeanor

In their book *Leadership Presence,* Belle Linda Halpern and Kathy Lubar define the quality of "presence" as the art of connecting authentically to an audience. That's a great way to think of your goal for a job interview: to connect authentically with the interviewer. I'll take it a step further by noting that you become "present" in the job interview—authentic, confident, and putting your best self forward—with a combination of professional demeanor, positive outward attitude, and relaxed state of mind.

You want to present an appealing image, but not a false one. Remember that you are making a commitment to the image you present, or else they'll say (with disappointment, usually), "She didn't seem like that in the interview!"

Here are some simple ways to project a professional demeanor:

- Speak clearly and slowly, and don't be afraid to pause and think about your answers to questions. If you need a minute to answer, say, "That's a great question! I am going to take a moment to think about it before I answer."
- Let your enthusiasm show. Carol Szatkowski, president of Clear Point Consultants, says that this attitude alone can separate you from your competition: "When a candidate is crystal clear, their energy is up, they're confident—that happens about once in every twenty-five interviews."
- Look the interviewer in the eyes as you answer.
- Try to balance your interview. If you've thoroughly discussed technical skills, for example, also include a story about your problem-solving capability.
- Project a positive attitude about your job search, previous jobs, schools, or experiences. Even if you have negative feelings, do not share them.
- Quietly keep your guard up. Some interviewers use confrontation or informality to get you to divulge information you otherwise would withhold.
- Here's a little mantra to repeat: "act warm, keep cool."

Conversely, avoid these red flags; experienced interviewers see them all as danger signs:

- Watch your language (even if your interviewer uses colorful or vulgar expressions). Likewise, avoid off-color jokes or sarcastic remarks about anything (even in small talk).

- Be direct and truthful about negative facts, such as why you were fired two jobs ago. Evasive or dishonest answers to questions are a killer.
- If you don't have anything to say, stop talking. Ask a question. Candidates who go on and on about nothing are not only weak, they're boring.
- Do not talk on a cell phone, listen to your MP3 player, fiddle with your PDA, or otherwise signal that there's something more important than this interview.
- Do not trash your previous employer. Ever. No company considering you wants to imagine that someday you'll leave and start bashing them.
- Avoid showing any negative attitudes—desperation, discouragement, annoyance, impatience, frustration, and so forth— even if you feel them.
- Be careful you don't fidget or put on that scared, deer-in-the-headlights expression.
- Don't show obvious appearance of illness, e.g., heavy sniffling (it's better to reschedule than have an interviewer distracted by trying to avoid your cold).
- Don't smoke or drink alcohol (even if invited). There are occasional exceptions to this rule but they are becoming rare in current business culture—a sign that the relationship is well established. In an interview, the relationship is just beginning.

Finally, three more subtle behaviors to avoid:

- Watch the difference between confidence and arrogance. If you are applying for a job, assume you *don't* know it all. Confident people aren't afraid of asking questions.
- Be careful of gestures like pointing, covering your mouth with a hand, or "mirroring" (subconsciously imitating the interviewer's posture).
- Avoid picking up the interviewer's accent (this is unconscious but very distracting).

You don't have to bury your personal style to project a professional demeanor. In fact, personal style is part of your fit with the job. Are you extroverted and excited to meet someone new? You don't have to hide that. Are you introverted and more interested in discussing the details of the job? It's fine to let that show.

The interviewer will notice the words you use to describe yourself, and that's where your preparation reveals the "real you." You might be curious, entrepreneurial, and passionate about success. You might be highly trustworthy, creative, provocative, easygoing, buttoned down, or enthusiastic. Since you don't know exactly which personal traits will appeal most to the interviewer, this is another time when telling the truth isn't just the right thing to do—it's the most effective as well.

## My Best Advice

No matter what skills and experience you're selling, you have to make an emotional connection with the buyer first. The best way to do this is to project your own feelings of excitement, enthusiasm, and a real passion for the work. Enthusiasm is infectious, and it leaves a lasting impression. We all know that certain skills or activities within a corporate environment can be taught, but it's hard for any manager to generate enthusiasm.

—*Presentation consultant Carmine Gallo*

## Listen Actively

Calvin Coolidge once said, "No man ever listened himself out of a job." The same is true of a job interview. To speak well, you have to listen well, and that means listening actively. You have two ears and one mouth. Use them proportionately.

Active listening is a habit of good interviewers (and good employees). It's a great contribution to your professional persona. It's also tactically powerful; often an amateur interviewer—such as a line manager—will talk for 90 percent of the interview. If they believe you've listened well, based on your questions and responses, they'll form a positive impression. Talkers love listeners.

To listen actively, do the following:

- Be mentally and physically ready to listen. Listening takes practice, so make it part of your rehearsal by having your partner ask some of the harder questions from chapters 6–10.
- Don't take over the interview with long monologues.
- Focus. Be alert to distractions. For example, the interviewer might sit between you and a large window. It's natural to look out the window as you talk, but you will look as if your mind is on other things.
- Clarify questions by rephrasing them. When you get an open-ended question, such as "Tell me about a time you improved results in your job," begin by saying, "Let me make sure I'm answering the right question. Would you like to know about a time I increased sales, or a time I streamlined one of our sales management procedures?" This answer shows you're listening and makes you a more interesting candidate.
- Refer at appropriate times to something the interviewer has said a few minutes before. This not only shows you're listening, but learning: "I'd like to tell you about my technical skills, especially in light of the new business plan you mentioned a few minutes ago. . . ."
- Take notes efficiently. If you think of a comment while an interviewer is talking, jot one or two words in your notebook. While note taking is expected most of the time, an interviewer's mind wanders if you scribble for a full minute.
- Conquer defensiveness. An interviewer might ask a stressful question to test your mettle. Instead of reacting defensively, tell yourself that they need more information before they make a judgment—clarify the question and answer it simply.
- Read the interviewer's behavior and role. Are they a talker or a listener? Is their job to check off a list of your skills and move you on to a second interview, or are they making deeper judgments about your character, motivation, and experience? Adjust your answers to fit their immediate task (it's fine to determine in advance what they want by asking, "What can I tell you today that would be most useful for your immediate task?").

- And as always, keep the attitude that you are there to learn as much about them as they are to learn about you. If you are genuinely interested in getting the right information, you will listen.

## Relax

"Just relax and be yourself" is easy to say and hard to do. Athletes and actors tell us the pressure to perform well is one of the chief hurdles that they have to overcome, and surrendering to a case of stage fright has killed many job interviews.

Nevertheless, peak performers on the stage or in sports invariably practice specific techniques for handling pressure or nervousness. Here are their suggestions:

- Talk back to your fears. When you think, "I'm a fraud, there's no way they'll hire me," say deliberately, "I am going to this interview because they believe I would be right for the job. I will impress them with a candid conversation about how well I can do this job."
- Breathe. A deep, slow breath relaxes your body, which in turn helps relax your mind. Some champion athletes deliberately yawn when the pressure builds. Try it (but not in front of the interviewer!).
- If you have learned affirmation or meditation techniques, use them the night before and the morning of your interview. In all their many varieties, these help you focus and "get out of your own way."
- Exercise. This isn't just for athletes or people trying to lose weight. Even gentle exercise, like walking the dog, raises your energy and your mood, and that produces a positive impression.
- Visualize a great performance. As an event approaches, I can see my greeting, and what the office will look like. I go over what will be said, planning the outcome hours or even days ahead of the event. I do this with meetings, speeches, new-product launches—even finding a parking space!
- Once you're in the interview, don't spend a lot of energy judg-

ing your performance. Focus your thinking on the immediate conversation—become truly interested in what the interviewer says and asks.

- If things go awry, don't take it too personally. Awkward or difficult interviews do happen, just as athletes and actors have off-nights. Maybe the interviewer is distracted or even hostile—that says more about him than it does about you. You can improve a lot by honestly evaluating an unpleasant interview experience, which makes it worthwhile.

Don't encourage stress. Keep your schedule open on the day of the interview (especially because they might ask you to stay longer—a wonderful sign!). Give yourself plenty of time to travel to the interview. Don't drink too much alcohol the night before or caffeine that morning. And as they tell kids in grade school—eat a good breakfast!

Perfection is the enemy of progress, so I'll conclude this section with one bit of counterintuitive advice: don't get *too* anxious about your appearance or the exact wording of your answers to interview questions. Interviewers understand that they are hiring a human being, and half their task is to discover the person underneath all the preparation. A confident job interview happens when you know you've prepared in the best ways possible. Then you can let go of being perfect and focus on showing as much of your talent, experience, and personality as you can. It not only feels good to do this; it is the best way to make a solid match between you and the job.

## Concluding the Interview

They've asked questions, you've asked questions. You like them, you hope they like you, and the interview is almost over. Near the close, the interviewer will say something like "Well, I have a 3 o'clock appointment, so we'll have to end in a moment." This is the moment for your closing argument to the jury.

*Thank you. I came to this interview intrigued by the job, and now I'm enthused about joining this wonderful organization.*

Then close with a very brief summary, and **if you like the job, ask for it.**

*You need the following skills [list them]. I have proven my skills with the accomplishments I described such as [name one]. I know enough to make a decision [or, I know enough to be enthusiastic about the job]. I believe we have a fit here. I can perform beyond your expectations. So please know this: I'm very interested in taking the next step, whether that's another interview, or an offer. Thanks!*

Then you shake hands, and go home.

And then you follow up.

## What Were They Thinking?

Several years ago, my place of business was located at 140 West 51st Street in New York City. A job applicant set up an appointment for 10:30 A.M., but when that time came, he didn't show up. Fifteen minutes later, he called to say he would be late because he went by mistake to 1240 West 51st Street instead of 140 West 51st Street.

I could not resist asking him, "How's the water today?" He seemed puzzled, until I explained that there is no such address as 1240 West 51st Street, because the last address before the Hudson River is in the 1100s. He then confessed that he simply had overslept. He was admittedly a very creative fellow and perhaps a good swimmer, but given the lack of honesty, we went on to the next applicant.

—*Anonymous recruiter*

## EXERCISE

## Interview Tip Sheet

Create a tip sheet like this and study it before each interview. Keep it handy during the interview as well, to remind you of points you want to make and questions you want to ask. I've stripped it down to the bare essentials, so it will even fit on an index card for a quick study moments before the interview. If you have practiced your presentation, you will need only a couple of words in each space to remind you what to say.

Company name: _____

Job title: _____

What the department does: _____

What the job does: _____

How success is measured: _____

Who would I report to (who's the boss): _____

My key messages (statements I must get across):

_____

_____

My key achievement stories for this job (two- or three-word reminders):

_____

Three questions I must ask: _____

_____

_____

**You can download this form at monstercareers.com.**

# 14  Follow Up!

For the third time, Michael read the e-mail he'd composed that afternoon on the bus ride home. The interview had gone well, and he'd already spent twenty minutes writing three thank-you notes. They lay in envelopes by the front door. Now it was 5:30 P.M., already dark, and Michael was tired. Mitch, who had been cooped up in the house all day, whined to go outside. Finish this e-mail, thought Michael, take Mitch for a walk, and stop at Earl's. Think about dinner later.

Michael decided the e-mail was right, and sent it on its way. Mitch jumped up as Michael rose to get the leash. Michael didn't bother to change out of his suit. On the way out, he grabbed the letters.

Twenty minutes later, across town, Patricia finished reading Michael's e-mail. She printed the attachment and forwarded Michael's e-mail to the others who had interviewed him that afternoon, adding the note, "As if you weren't already impressed with this guy, take a look at the attached. I think we have a winner. Please reply by close of business tomorrow and I'll put together an offer."

The last phase of the interview process is like crossing on thin ice: If you stop before you're on the other side, you'll fall into cold water and disappear. You have to keep in motion, and following up after the interview keeps you moving forward. A candidate who follows up with interviewers can overcome competition with more experience, more skills, or a smoother interview style. The reason is simple: follow-up continues the relationship.

It's amazing how few candidates follow up well . . . or at all. They think, "Okay, that employer has seen what I've got, so now the ball's in their court," and then they go completely passive. Soon the old rejection anxiety kicks in: "If I follow up too much they'll get sick of me bugging them." So they sit tight. Time passes, the interviewer gets busy with his or her job, and the candidate just . . . fades . . . away. . . .

This is not the way to get a job! Without follow-up, you're sitting in "The Waiting Place" that Dr. Seuss described in his wonderful book, *Oh, the Places You'll Go!* Nothing happens in the waiting place.

Consider the impression *not* following up creates: Maybe you're not really interested in the job. Maybe you lack persistence. Maybe you just forgot. Maybe you lack the self-confidence to speak up. Believe me, those are not qualities that generate enthusiasm in a potential employer!

Start your follow-up the day of the interview—ideally before the close of business. At least, determine that you won't go to sleep that night before making your first follow-up move.

## What to Say

Once again, let's take a lesson from sales managers, who actually ask candidates to follow up an interview with:

- A brief summary of the meeting.
- What the candidate learned.
- What the candidate wanted the manager to learn.
- A suggestion for the next step.

Smart sales candidates know that this is just like following up on a sales call.

So, tell your interviewers what you learned, what they learned, and ask for the job. For example, state that you think the job is just right because of something the interviewer told you about the company—an impending product change, a restructuring, a big problem you're being hired to solve. (See the follow-up letters at the end of this chapter for effective conclusion statements.)

If you had multiple interviews, treat each interviewer as an individual. Send a separate communication to each, recalling your individual conversation. (Does this seem like too much work? That depends on whether or not you're willing to out-hustle your competition for the job.)

## How to Say It

Of course you'll send a thank-you note, because you genuinely appreciate the time you've been given . . . but just in case you need more reasons to say thanks, career counselor Peter Vogt suggests five:

1. By sending a thank-you note, you show your interviewer common courtesy and respect.
2. Many other candidates won't send a note; you automatically stand out if you do.
3. A thank-you note gives you an opportunity to reiterate points you made during your interview.
4. A thank-you note lets you make points you forgot to make in your interview.
5. A thank-you note demonstrates your written communication skills.

Candidates spend a lot of energy worrying about format—e-mail or letter? Formal or informal? Handwritten or typed? Phone call before or after the e-mail? The fact is the format matters less to most interviewers than what you say, but here are some differences to consider:

A **handwritten note** demonstrates a personal touch, and there's a "sticky" quality to one—they're hard to throw out. Often they're placed right in the file with your resume. If you're going to send a note, use the classiest stationery or note card you can afford. Include a business card, even if you left one behind at the interview.

A **typed letter** in business format projects a professional image. It is best for notes that go beyond thanks. Show that you paid close attention by expanding on an important discussion point, adding a brief achievement story, or adding information you needed to check during the interview.

**E-mail** is the quickest, most convenient follow-up method, but also the most easily forgotten. Use e-mail to quickly say thanks, I had a great time, I'm really interested, and I'll be in touch soon—and send it the day of the interview. E-mail is also a good format to use if the employer requested supplemental information in electronic form (such as references).

**Phone calls** produce mixed results. They're easy for interviewers to avoid, yet they have an urgent quality that can become annoying. If you want to call to follow up, it's best to ask for permission at the close of the interview. You might also want to use the phone for a quick "ping," reminding the interviewer (after you send the written follow-up) that you're still available and interested.

From the employer's point of view, each format has a different degree of "pressure to respond." Handwritten notes and business letters don't require a reply (but often get one). An e-mail raises the "reply" pressure a bit. A phone call raises it more because they have to decide whether to take the call. (Incidentally, I don't suggest you show up in the lobby demanding to see them, unless you want them to call security!)

If you are unsure which format to use, it's perfectly fine to say at the end of an interview, "This job sounds great and I've enjoyed talking to you. I always like to follow up and, knowing you're busy, I'll ask, do you prefer letters, e-mail, or a call?" Be aware that many recruiters have strict filters on their e-mail (in part to protect from computer viruses), so if they prefer e-mail, confirm that it will reach them. Don't forget to collect business cards with e-mail addresses and phone numbers.

Actually, you don't have to settle on a single format in most cases. Instead, take advantage of the number of formats available to make multiple light touches. Here's a sample follow-up schedule using multiple formats.

- Day of the interview—e-mail thank-you note.
- Within one business day—handwritten thank-you note.
- Within one week of the interview—follow-up letter (either e-mail or business letter) repeating thanks, adding "one more thing that might interest you."
- Within ten days of the interview—phone call asking how their search is going, confirming your interest, and asking if you might add anything.

This steady, low-pressure follow-up reminds interviewers of you even as they see other candidates. The freshness of an impression diminishes very rapidly, and you can't help the fact that you might be only a pleasant memory a week after the face-to-face meeting. Your follow-up reminds them of not only your interest in them, but all the reasons they should be interested in you.

## My Best Advice

I knew a candidate who wasn't right for a certain job, but after the interview, he followed up with me on a consistent basis. He sent a handwritten note every few months. He followed up even after he found a temporary job at another company, saying, "This is where I'm working now, but it's temporary so keep me in mind." He was low-key and sincere; he didn't intrude on my time, yet he still reminded me consistently of his interest. That's memorable!

—*Amy Needleman, MarketSource Corp.*

Eventually you will get one of three replies: "yes," "no," or "come back for more." The third, being called back for more interviews, means they have a positive impression and either need to know more or need to have additional people meet you. In this case, you need to circle back to your preparation mode, rehearse some new achievement stories, put what you learned into customizing your next interview more closely to the employer's circumstances, and go get 'em!

"Yes" and "No" replies trigger new activity.

## Yes—The Job Offer

You got the job offer! Now, instead of selling yourself, you're buying (the decision is yours, not theirs). Is this the right organization, the right job, and the right offer? Did you like the people you met, and are you convinced the business is a good one? Did anything you learn make you uneasy? If so, you need to ask clarifying questions before you say, yes, great, I'll take the job.

What salary, benefits, and working conditions have they offered? You can express great enthusiasm for the job offer while filling gaps in your knowledge about the job or the organization. There is almost always room to negotiate an offer that is a little more closely tailored to your absolute ideal situation.

You might have to decline an offer. Perhaps you really cannot afford to earn what they can afford to pay. Perhaps the interview process raised enough red flags about the company's personnel, culture, or prospects that you just feel uneasy about taking the job. In a hot job market, you may believe you can do better. It takes courage and integrity to decline an offer that seems wrong, but it can also be a great service to your career, your peace of mind and, in the long run, your wallet. If the job's not right, if the offer's not right . . . politely and respectfully decline, then get on with your search for the perfect job!

## Yes . . . Yes . . . Yes—Multiple Offers!

Have you received more than one offer in a short time span? Multiple offers are a dream situation for the candidate, because several employers are bidding for your services—it looks a lot like an auction in which every part of the "winning bid" is negotiable. Go with the big company for greater benefits or the small company where you'll have more responsibility? Take the job with flexible work hours, or the one that's twenty miles closer to home? Play the auction game to get the most money, or leverage the interest of multiple players to get just a little more out of the organization offering your dream job? All these factors are in play, and within the limits of what the market can afford to pay for your services, multiple offers give you more power to design exactly the job you want.

Multiple offers don't always happen . . . but they never happen by accident. They're a result of intense activity all along the road you've traveled in your job search. Here are ways to encourage two or three offers coming within a few days of each other:

- Multiple offers start as multiple touches. Focus your touches, leads, and send-outs on several organizations at once—I'd say at least twenty for touches and ten for leads. If you're interviewing at three places simultaneously, you've been busy!
- Keep networking, researching, and learning about new opportunities, even as you prepare for an interview.
- Intensify activity around job opportunities that are hot. If you've been called in for a third round of interviews somewhere, let others know with a polite phone message: "This is Jeff. I understand if you haven't made a decision but I wanted you to know that I'm very excited about this job, and another company has asked me in for a final round of interviews. I'd hate to lose the opportunity with you just because of an accident of timing."
- Continue actively reaching out even when you sense an offer is on its way. Many factors out of your control can delay an offer, but you can use that delay to "heat up" other possibilities.

Negotiating multiple offers is a high-stakes game, and one employer might deal a hard hand: "This is the offer; it's good for forty-eight hours only. Yes or no?" Don't think this attitude means you cannot negotiate. You can contact the other employers and say you have an offer and you must respond quickly. If they want you, they'll respond. If they say they want you but cannot make a job offer . . . well, how do you feel about turning down a solid offer in favor of a vague intention?

A word of caution: Don't bluff in this game. If you don't have another offer, don't say you do. You'll end up either getting the job under false pretences (and being fired for it) or having the offer withdrawn.

## No—Someone Else Got the Job!

They want someone else. It's humbling, frustrating, humiliating—you knew you had the job down cold and then you didn't get it. Maybe someone else came along who had more experience; many times the successful candidate was just a better fit culturally. If the recruiter or manager is doing a good job, there's always a choice at the end. Someone gets selected, and sometimes there's little difference between candidates.

Getting defensive or angry at this point is a big mistake. Smile, say thank you, and stay professional. There might be another opening next week.

If you do not get a job offer, there's still a use for follow-up: you can make a positive impression (and improve your job search) by asking for feedback. Don't ask what you did wrong. Ask, "What could I have improved upon? What in my experience, presentation, or skills would have been more convincing?" Be prepared to hear the truth about your performance. This is valuable information when you prepare for your next interview.

Most HR departments have policies against giving out interview information, so perhaps only one out of four interviewers will give you any real feedback, but you should ask anyway. A hiring manager might be more receptive to the request. If a third-party recruiter was involved, ask them. Some interviewers will give a candidate honest feedback. I do.

Carole Martin, author of *Boost Your Interview IQ*, offers six rules to follow when asking for feedback:

1. Be sure to relay your disappointment in not getting the offer and say that you would be interested in interviewing again if anything opens up. Emphasize that this company is still your top choice.

2. Politely ask if there is any feedback that would help you improve your chances in your next interview. Was there anything in particular that could have helped your chances of winning the job offer?
3. Listen carefully to any advice and take notes. Do not argue or defend yourself. You are asking for feedback, not a chance for a rebuttal.
4. Keep your discussion short. Ask one or two follow-up questions, and then end the conversation.
5. Thank your interviewer for the feedback and the chance to improve your skills. Reiterate that if another opening comes up, you would be interested in interviewing.
6. Take the advice given and think about changing some of your techniques to improve your next interview.

Even if you don't get the job, thoughtful follow-up leaves a positive impression. You continue a relationship that might lead to a job in a month. You might add the interviewer(s) to your personal network, and find them recruiting you five years from now!

Stay positive because the employer's first choice might decline the offer. What if you're the second or third choice? Any manager who's been hiring for a few years can tell you about the second- or third-choice candidate who turned out to be a superior employee, a leader in the company, and a joy to work with. Maybe you'll be that person for your next manager.

Finally, follow up with yourself. How could you have performed better? Did you run out of achievement stories? Memorize two or three new ones. Did you apply for the right level of job? Did you learn anything that could improve your performance in the next interview? Don't agonize with "I should have said. . . ." Instead, tell yourself, "Next time, I'll say the following. . . ."

## Sample Follow-up Letters

### *Business Letter (with Enclosure)*

Mr. Paul McGill
VP, Finance and Operations
The Open Hand School
5555 Main Street
Columbus, OH

Dear Mr. McGill:

Thank you again for such an interesting discussion of the product-planning position at the Open Hand School today. I hope you could tell from my questions how excited I am to be considered for the job.

While all of our conversation was helpful, I'd particularly like to point out the similarities between the new product development plan you mentioned and my successful introduction of three Web-based products at Round Table, Inc., in the last eighteen months. There's no room for wishful thinking in a product management position, so you're right to be looking for someone with a "trust, but verify" attitude about every detail during the development process.

As promised, I enclose a copy of a note of thanks sent to me by a department head a few months ago, which I hope confirms in your mind my attitude of giving my internal "customers" exceptional service—of *listening* to them.

Once again, I think I'd do very well by Open Hand, and I'm excited by the prospect of working with you and your team. I look forward to hearing from you.

Sincerely,
*Leslie Parker*
Leslie Parker

/enc.

# E-mail with Attachment

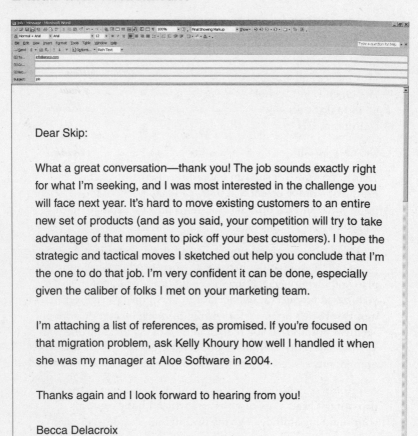

Dear Skip:

What a great conversation—thank you! The job sounds exactly right for what I'm seeking, and I was most interested in the challenge you will face next year. It's hard to move existing customers to an entire new set of products (and as you said, your competition will try to take advantage of that moment to pick off your best customers). I hope the strategic and tactical moves I sketched out help you conclude that I'm the one to do that job. I'm very confident it can be done, especially given the caliber of folks I met on your marketing team.

I'm attaching a list of references, as promised. If you're focused on that migration problem, ask Kelly Khoury how well I handled it when she was my manager at Aloe Software in 2004.

Thanks again and I look forward to hearing from you!

Becca Delacroix

## Handwritten Note

> Dear Susan:
>
> I was very pleased to talk with you today about the facilities management job. I had not expected to end up discussing how raising money for a day school is like managing office buildings!
>
> I hope our conversation told you that I'm right for the job. I'm certainly convinced I could make a great contribution, so thank you for taking the time to talk.
>
> Sincerely,
>
> Dave

## What Were They Thinking?

I was a 24-year-old recruiter on my first job. One day, I was a few minutes into an interview with a young woman when she asked me if she could bring her baby into my office. She had left her baby in the waiting room!

She brought the baby in. He was fidgety. All of a sudden, there's an awful smell in my office—the baby's diaper is not on very well! The poor woman tried to clean it up but made a horrendous mess. The facilities staff had to come down, take out the chairs, and shampoo the rug. My administrative assistant was laughing to the point of tears. Remember, I was just a kid. I'd never seen a dirty diaper. I was floored, baffled, and mortified.

About two days later, I get a call from the woman, and she says, "Can I still be considered for the job?"

—*HR executive at a Fortune 500 company*

Ten years ago, I interviewed an executive assistant named Kaycee Langford. I really wanted her to join my team, but Monster at the time consisted of barely a dozen people working above a Chinese restaurant in a strip mall, and Kaycee had a secure job offer from a large, successful toy company. So I asked, "Two years into this job, do you want to be making plastic toys, or do you want to be helping me change the world?" It may be the smartest interview question I ever asked. Kaycee has played a critical role in my work life and in Monster's success since that day.

Everything in this book, from the interview questions to the advice on following up after an interview, is dedicated to helping you get to that moment, because your work life really is that important. Whether your goal is to support your family, or get your career off on the right track, or retire early, or pursue your dreams for a better world, I hope you take your job that seriously.

If you're like most people, your work will occupy about one-third of your life. That's what I call a commitment! And so, before you make that commitment, put in the time it takes to land the job of your life. If you haven't done the exercises in this book, go back and do them. Study the interview questions. Give yourself the advantage of a little extra preparation, a little extra dedication to landing in the right place. You'll be glad you did. And you just might change the world.

# MONSTER QUESTION INDEX